Dear Reader:

What can I say about CP Time? I have been guilty of it, I have been victimized by it, I have been angered by it, and I have been amused by it. Rarely do I attend an event organized by people of color that starts on time, including my own events. I admit it. No matter how much you plan in advance, something seems to always come up to cause a setback or a delay.

When it comes to getting someplace on time, something as little as a phone call can make you late, or waiting for your sweater to dry, or having to stop for gas before you end up on the side of the road with an empty tank. Then there are those who simply cannot seem to get anywhere or do anything on time. That is what this book is about; examining why it happens.

So join *New York Times* Bestselling Author J.L. King for an entertaining and provocative look at CP Time. I have a feeling that most people will see themselves in more than a few of these situations and many others that they know. This is a fun book to discuss with your friends and family members, your coworkers, even your kids.

Thanks for the support of this book and all the other Strebor titles. If you have a CP Time story that you wish to share—possibly for a future volume—please email it to CPTime@streborbooks.com.

Stay Blessed and Be on Time,

Zane

Zane
Publisher
Strebor Books International
www.streborbooks.com

ZANE PRESENTS

CP TIME

J.L. KING

ZANE PRESENTS

CP TIME

Why Some People Are Always Late

J.L. King

SBI

Strebor Books
New York London Toronto Sydney

Published by
SBI
Strebor Books
P.O. Box 6505
Largo, MD 20792
http://www.streborbooks.com

This book is a work of fiction. Names, characters, places and incidents are products of the author's imagination or are used fictitiously. Any resemblance to actual events or locales or persons, living or dead, is entirely coincidental.

Cover Design: www.mariondesigns.com
Illustrations: XCreations by Xavier Daniels

ISBN-13 978-1-59309-108-8
ISBN 1-59309-108-7
LCCN 2006938896

First printing: February 2007

10 9 8 7 6 5 4 3 2 1

Manufactured in the United States of America

For information regarding special discounts for bulk purchases, please contact Simon & Schuster Special Sales at 1-800-456-6798 or business@simonandschuster.com

I dedicate this book to everyone
who has ever had to wait on anyone who is always late!

ACKNOWLEDGMENTS

To my God, who is my literary agent, and always shows up on time in my life.

I would like to thank everyone who gave me their favorite CP Time story and to a few close friends and family members who are not always late, but they mean a lot to me, they are:

Brenda Stone Browder, thank you for your input on this book. I appreciate you.

Ebony M. King, my daughter, I hope you will stop being late after you read this book.

James B. King, my son, thank God you don't live your life on CP Time, but your return calls are on CP Time; work on that, please.

Loren Browder III, thanks for allowing us to use your image on the cover of this book. I hope it will jumpstart your modeling career.

To the current love of my life, (I will not mention a name), thank you for your support as I worked on this book into the wee hours of the morning, and didn't give you your time.

To my parents, the late Mr. and Mrs. Louis V. (Lillie Mae) King who were never late for anything, and raised my brother, Ronald L. King, and I, to always be on time.

And last but not least, to Zane and the Strebor publishing team, for believing in this book. Thank you for all of your support.

CONTENTS

INTRODUCTION

Time has caused many people to have major health problems, and even untimely death. People who are living by every tick-tock of a timepiece are constantly stressed out, counting every second. We all know that stress can kill. These people are stressed out because they chronically rush to beat time, which causes stress on their heart to beat faster, which could lead to high blood pressure, a heart attack, or stroke. People who try hard to be perfect in everything they do, including being on time, let time control their every minute.

These people are not procrastinators. They make things happen: they are the first one at the meeting, at church, at the dinner, the social affair; you can count on them to be there. They arrive minutes early to make sure to be on time. People who are clock watchers know when that second hand hits the last minute of their work day, they are out of their places of employment so fast, that many hit the mark seconds after their quitting time. People who make a habit of being on time have little patience for those who are not.

People sometimes lose their patience at the grocery store because the line is too long or the cashier is taking her "good old time." They see red when they pay their hard-earned money to attend a play, movie, or concert, only to have the "curtain time" late. They complain, "It must be black folk running this show; when black folk are involved, events do not begin on time. Black folk are always on *CP Time* for everything." These are statements from black people, mind you. According to many people, all black people are late for everything. This type of self-absorbed thinking that *they* are the only black folk who are always on time, exists because they have the misconception of being perfect, and everything they do is in order.

One may ask why would I want to write a book about *CP Time*, after writing two bestselling books about sexuality and relationships? Most people know me as "Mr. DL," or "That man who was on *Oprah*." Well, this is what happened that created this book that you are reading:

I was at a party in Houston, Texas last year. The party was a combination of two events: A book signing for me, and a celebration for my friend who kicked off a new clothing line for women. He had sent out his invitations three weeks in advance, and requested that his invited guest RSVP for the event. The event was scheduled to start at 7 p.m. He had the caterer at his home four hours before the party was to begin, and the food (a full buffet) was on the table and ready to go.

I had arrived on time, at 8 p.m.; none of the other guests had arrived. The host, bartender, and the caterer were at the party. At 9 p.m., still no guests. By this time, the caterer blew out the Sterno candles, which were keeping the chicken wings, meatballs, and other finger foods warm. The bartender was passing the time, sitting on the back patio talking on the phone, and my friend was pacing back and forth.

He repeated over and over, "You know how black folk are. Tell them seven, and they show up at eleven." He kept looking out of the window, checking his watch and trying to save face with me. In his mind, I am this big-superstar celebrity and my time was too valuable to be wasted waiting on his guests.

Shortly after 9 p.m., the doorbell rang. His first guest had arrived. As this person walked in, he didn't apologize for being late, he just came in, greeted everyone and sent to the bar for a drink. Other guests continued to arrive until midnight.

While mixing and mingling with my friend's guests, I engaged in a conversation with a sister who taught at the University of Houston. I asked her, "Why is it that we never start on time for anything?"

She replied, that it is just who we are, and as much as we complain about it, we simply deal with it. She then said to me, "Someone needs to write a book about *CP Time*; I would make it a mandatory read for my black studies class. It would be a good book for other ethnic students to read, because they don't understand the behavior."

I expressed to her my desire to write a book about *CP Time*. She said, "If you do, let me know, so that I can order copies."

I returned to Atlanta and began my research to see if anyone had ever written a book about *CP Time*. I googled *CP Time*, and colored peoples time: no results, blank, zero, nada, nothing had been written as a book. There were some books that mentioned it, but no real look at it. So I decided to write a book about *CP Time*. I wanted it to be humorous and light, as well as educational and informative.

The first thing I needed to do was talk to friends, family members, associates, and strangers, to gather their favorite *CP Time* story and their feelings about *CP Time*. I hired a sister from Washington, D.C. to canvass the Howard University campus area to randomly gather *CP Time* stories from people. We also established a web site, and requested people to submit their favorite *CP Time* stories. Well, we received hundreds of e-mails, and the sister gathered numerous funny stories from her "street" interviews. Many people she spoke to agreed that a book about *CP Time* would be great.

That is how this book got started, and after several months of writing, I am happy I can provide you with a look at a behavior that has driven all of us crazy. I personally try really hard on not being on *CP Time*, but I'm guilty of arriving at parties and events on *CP Time* for various reasons that I tell you about in the next chapter. So, writing this book has helped me take a look at my own lateness and I am going to work on doing better. But, the truth of the matter is that I try to be fifteen minutes *early* for everything that I am invited to. (Sometimes I am, and sometimes I'm late.) I don't know if I'm this way about being early because of the time I spent in the military for eight years, or my intolerance for having to wait on people (I don't want them waiting on me), or because I was raised by my parents to be on time. But, whatever it is about me that gives me inspiration to always set a goal to be on time, I can't get around the fact, that most of my family and friends are always on *CP Time*. The worst case of *CP Time* that directly affects my life is my daughter Ebony; she is always on *CP Time* (more about Miss Ebony later).

I hope you enjoy this book. I am contemplating writing several volumes. While reading it, you will probably not want to put it down, but please DO NOT MAKE YOURSELF LATE!

Enjoy, and always be on time for something!

JL King

THE AUTHOR'S  OWN *CP TIME* PROBLEM

Although I am writing a book about *CP Time*, which is one of my pet peeves, I have to be honest and admit that I also have been guilty of *CP Time*. Even though I try to arrive early to events, affairs and engagements, there have been a few times (more than a few) when I was on *CP Time*.

I make a conscious effort to arrive on *CP Time* to parties. I hate to be the first one there. I will wait one to two hours after the party is to start. I will sit in my car, and wait until I see other people go into the house or club. I will drive around and even have taken magazines or books to read while waiting in the car because I didn't want to be the first one to arrive. Even at my own affairs, I have arrived late, to make an "entrance."

Once I hosted an art reception for one hundred-fifty people. The invitations stated that the reception hosted by J.L. King started at 7 p.m., however, I didn't arrive until 7:45 p.m. I had the audacity to call my host and ask him how many people, and who had arrived. I love making that "fashionably late" entrance...it can be a rush. So, I can't point four fingers at those who have been on *CP Time*, because I am guilty also.

EST. CST. MST. PST. CP Time

CHAPTER ONE

WHAT IS CP TIME?

IN THIS SECTION I WILL EXPLORE TIME, **in the beginning**, and the impact of God, or how a higher power in your life can make being late a lifesaver or life-changing event.

When I began working on this book, I posed the questions to a very close friend, "What is the meaning of time? Who came up with the word 'time,' and is time defined the same by everyone?"

To find answers I logged on to one of the web search engines and typed in the word *time*. I got hundreds of links, and had many ways to get as much information about time that my brain could conceive. You can find anything you want about time: What is the meaning of time? What is the concept of time? What is time management? Who invented time? What does the word "time" mean? How does time work? Universal time, time quotes, and does time really exist, were just a few of the search engines that I discovered about time.

Timing is everything. It's good to have a beautiful coat, hat and gloves, but not in the summer! The Bible speaks about seasons and knowing how to number your days! If you are always late for work or appointments, it sends a definite signal. Remember, tardiness is silent rebellion! BE ON TIME.

(Taken from the book Words of Wisdom, Daily Affirmations of Faith *by Rev Run. AMISTAD, an Imprint of Harper Collins Publishers)*

In my research I discovered that the very first clock was a sundial, and that form of time keeping had been used for over five thousand years. The Chaldeans, and Sumerians, in Babylonia, used the first sundials (which was a part of the modern Iraq). That is some deep stuff.

I wondered if the Chaldeans or Sumerians had any brothers or sisters who lived on *CP Time*. I can visualize it now: it is 500,000 B.C. and the earth is shifting; the glaciers are forming the Great Lakes and the Rocky Mountains; the chief of the Chaldeans put out a message that the tribe needed to move to higher land, and there is a *brother* who is always late. He oversleeps and misses the evacuation of the village to safer land. When he wakes up, he realizes that because of his always being late, he missed out, and now is about to have his ass frozen for future generations to look at as the well-preserved prehistoric caveman. The one that you heard was discovered in the Antarctic was probably a brother who was late, and ended up getting tracked and frozen. This gives you something to think about...?

As I was doing my research I wondered if since the beginning of mankind, were there people who were always late? That really made writing this chapter really interesting. And I have to admit I learned a great amount of information, which aroused my curiosity further.

But, this book is about *CP Time* and why some people are always late. However, I wanted to give you a little insight on time. As they say, you don't know where you are going, if you don't know where you've been…and of course knowledge is power. So, now you have been exposed a little about the history of time. Next time you are playing Jeopardy, you might get a couple of points if there is a category about time.

WHAT IS CP TIME?

CP Time has been defined many different ways as I discovered while writing this book. In *How to Be, A Guide to Contemporary Living for African Americans* by Harriette Cole (Simon & Schuster, 2000) she writes: *CP Time* is defined as "chronic lateness."

Another book, by Geneva Smitherman, *Black Talk: Words and Phrases from the Hood to the Amen Corner* (Mariner Books, 2000), states that *CP Time* was a reference to the African American concept of time, being in tune with human events, nature, the seasons, and natural rhythms as opposed to being a slave to the clock, which represents artificial, rather then natural, time.

Donald McCullough, a white author who didn't use the term *CP Time*, wrote in *Say Please, Say Thank You* (Perigee Books, 1999) that people who are late, may as well be guilty of stealing time. Time is something that cannot be wasted. This author also writes that people who are late have said, in effect that their time is more valuable then your time, and that what you are doing is not as important as what I am doing, and that you do not mind stealing fifteen minutes of my day to squander on your own purposes.

Even the Ms. Emily Post, the etiquette queen of many books on how to live a life being proper, said that people who are late are out and out TACKY (she didn't use that word, but that is what she wanted to say.)

No matter how you define it, it is a behavior that has two sides, the good and the bad.

Late...again?!!!

CHAPTER TWO

CP Time Social

? *What* TIME DOES A PARTY/EVENT REALLY BEGIN, and why are people who live there on CP *Time*?

? *Why* IS IT THAT NO ONE WANTS TO BE THE FIRST ONE TO ARRIVE, which feeds into people being on CP *Time*?

? *Who* ARE THE WORST WHEN IT COMES TO ARRIVING TO SOCIAL GATHERINGS, men or women and why?

ALL EYES ON ME

I am ashamed to say my friends, and family members know me for being on "*CPT.*" No matter how hard I try, I'm always late. When I do arrive on time, people think they're late and question the time because they know how I am. However, I've made up a perfectly good reason for my lateness. I like to consider my *CP Time* "fashionably late." **I like to make an entrance. I like for all eyes to be on me when I walk in the room.** I know I'm so self-absorbed, but I must admit I love it. Now grant it, they may just be talking about me wondering why I'm just getting there, but I like to think that they are more focused on how extravagant I look. It's bad and every year I make my New Year's resolution to work on my lateness. I can say it's gotten better but it still happens more often than not.

But to defend myself, sometimes there are things that go on that cause my lateness, which I have no control over. There is that unforeseen traffic jam; people being nosey because someone has gotten pulled over. There's the weather, there's that one day you had a wild night and have no idea where your keys are, let alone where your car is. There are a million and one excuses of unpreventable lateness.

"Everything I do, no matter what it is, I'm always on CP Time. I'm late for work, I eat late, I stay up late, I have sex late, I was born late and I will probably die late. I guess being late is in my nature. The only thing that I am on time for is my period; and if that is late, then I'm all messed up."

On the contrary, I make it a point to be on time for business and interviews. There's no excuse for being late to those types of things. Now I can't promise you that I'll ever be early again but I try. So to wrap it all up, it's an attention thing for me. What can I say? I'm one of seven, and I strive for the attention. So I blame my mother for my lateness. After all, she passed it down to me.

> **CP Time is when you want to have a gathering or party start at 3:00 p.m., you have to put on the invitation 1:00 p.m. so everybody will be at the event by 3:00 p.m. I am an Event Planner and I did a baby shower and I had to send out two different invitations: one for on-time guests and another for CP Time guests. CP Time is real, and I deal with it daily when planning events...**
> **It is something that most of us are very proud of...I always get, 'Girl, you know I am always on CP Time...'**

LET THE SHOW START

Why is it that entertainers who are scheduled to start performing on time are always late? I had VIP tickets to see a jazz artist. The show was promoted to start at 9 p.m. There was no opening act, just her. Well, at 10 p.m. the show had not started, at 11 p.m. the show had not started, and at midnight, no show. I was pissed and everybody in the auditorium was getting angry. The Master of Ceremonies kept coming out telling the crowd that when the show did start it was going to be *all of that*. Well, at a little after midnight the band came out on stage and started warming up. This didn't help the matter any, because they took over thirty minutes to set up and warm up.

When the artist finally came out to start the concert, she received a very warm welcome, however, most of the crowd had left. The only reason my date and I waited on her to start the show, was that we were told we'd get to go back stage and meet her. Well, after the show, we waited to be escorted back to her dressing room to get a picture taken with her. Her manager came out and told us that she was not feeling well, and that we could not see her. Well, I *went off* on the manager. I told him that we waited over three hours for the show to start. He said to me as calmly as he could..."Well *bro*, you know how performers are, they always start on CP Time, you should know that if you attend concerts." What BS.

HAPPY BIRTHDAY PARTY GONE BAD

In April, I attended a planned and highly publicized birthday dinner for a colleague at a local Atlanta restaurant—her curious nature prevented the would-be surprise gathering from being just that—guests were told to arrive at 7 p.m. on a warm Friday evening. The restaurant, located in one of the busiest areas of town, was popular among "YBUPs" (young, black, urban professionals) and was certain to be greatly patronized on this night. In anticipation, I opted to arrive a mere fifteen minutes early to ensure my prompt arrival, if only the birthday girl had the same respect for her guests as we did for her!!! Some of the 30 guests assembled by 7:45 p.m. had finished their third drink by this time and were becoming agitated (rightly so) and questioning the whereabouts of the honoree. In all of my years of knowing her, I've never known her to be on time for anything. We often joke that we'll have her to sleep at the church following her wedding rehearsal to be certain that she is there on time for her nuptials. At any rate, I decided to contact her cell phone to track her location. She didn't answer, however sent me a text message immediately following my call. The message read, "I can't answer the phone right now because I just put a *relaxer* in my hair & need to wash it out. Has anyone gotten to the restaurant yet?" Needless to say, everyone was highly upset that she was nowhere near ready to join us to celebrate her birthday. The crowd quickly ordered and had a wonderful dinner, conversation and atmosphere. Wouldn't you know, as we paid our tabs, in walks the birthday girl!!! No one said a word... I, and many others present, have not spoken with her since.

YOU KNOW HOW I DO IT

I'm always late, because my friends know that is who I am. My saying is, "You know how I do it." My friends know to not count on me to be on time. It ain't going to happen. **Either you like it, or you will get over it, if you want to be my friend.** I don't care if you do get upset with me, you will get over it. I don't care if I do make you wait or miss the opening of the movie, you will get over it. I don't care if you have to wait on me to arrive, you will get over it, because as my favorite saying goes..."You know how I do it."

LATE FOR THE CLUB

My best friend Sherrie is always, always late. We know this and often deal with her by giving her false times or by meeting her at the appointed place. One night in particular I, and our two other girlfriends, met at her house for cocktails before going out. We had made plans all week to go to this new club for all-night dancing. We all loved to dance. We all had not hung out together in a while, so it was going to be a "girls night out" of fun, men, and good music, and of course, lots of dancing. When we got to Sherrie's house, she answered the door in her robe and told us to come in to have a drink, and she would be right down. Well, we started drinking, talking, and playing catch-up, before we realized two hours had passed, but Sherrie had still not come downstairs. I go to her bedroom and knock on her door, and she opened the door fully dressed with a perm in her hair. After rinsing, drying, and gelling her hair, we finally arrive at the club at 2 a.m. When we got to the club there was still a line outside, so we had to stand in line. When we finally got to the front door, the security man tells us that the club is closing at 3 a.m. It is now 2:45 a.m. Well, we didn't go in, and we didn't get to dance, all because Sherrie wanted her hair to be right. She knew that we had made these plans in advance, and she still had us waiting on her. Sherrie is the prime example of *CP Time* at its worst or best.

ALWAYS ON TIME, NO MATTER WHAT

I have many friends who plan birthday parties for their children months in advance. They discuss these parties over the phone with me, ask my advice on themes for the party, and call requesting me to bring food, ice, or drinks. The day before the party I receive the invitation in the mail. Once I even received an invitation once I was at the party because the mom had forgotten to mail them on time. If a *CP* says the party starts at 2 p.m. you can best believe that it won't get started until 3:30 p.m.! I am strict about schedules; if I say 2 p.m., I'm ready at 2 p.m. The worst part about it is that *CPs* assume everyone else is like them so they will show up late for my planned party after I've put food away and expect me to pull everything out to feed them and their children!

What happened to the saying, "the early bird catches the worm"?

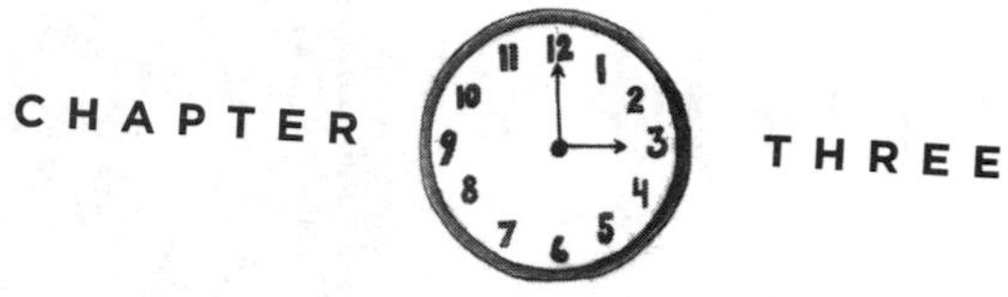

CHAPTER THREE

CP Time at Funerals

THERE IS NO EXCUSE on why some black people are always late. The fact of the matter is that they have no respect for time. They want people to see them as **the stars of the show** even though their names are not on the billboard. They want everybody to say their outfit is tight. Their hair is laid. They got it going on.

I think some black people are brought up in a society where it is accepted and most times expected that we will be late. As for myself, I run late many times because I know my trifling friends won't be on time. I heard people say such and such is going to be late for his own funeral. Now that is a damn shame, but there is some validity in the context of the statement. We mean well, but we are who we are...just late for everything.

OPEN UP THE CASKET

Anyone who would show up at a funeral on CP Time has a serious problem with being on time.

When my dad died, his brother and sister were late for the homegoing service. We had already shut the casket and the service had started. They come walking in, and had the nerve to ask if we would open up the casket so they could have a final look.

They knew what time the funeral was scheduled to start, they were driving from another city about four hours away, and were invited to come down the day before and stay with family, but they decided to drive down the day of the funeral service. And they showed up on *CP Time.*

When my brother told them no, that we were not going to open up the casket, my aunt got upset. She got upset because she was on *CP Time*, and we should understand that at least she was here, and why not? Well, she didn't get an opportunity to see her brother, and the service moved on.

I met a funeral home director in Houston, Texas who told me that he has had to deal with funerals starting late for many reasons. One of the funniest was when the mother of the deceased wanted to stop at K-mart on the way to the church to get a blouse.

The one she had on didn't match her shoes, and she didn't want to show up at the church not looking right. She insisted that the limo driver stop at the local K-mart and let her go in and pick up a blouse. She told him that she would not be long. Well, because she was on *CP Time* she ended up taking over forty-five minutes looking for a blouse.

In the meantime, at the church, everyone was waiting on the family. And the family was in the limousine, in the parking lot waiting on mother to pick out a blouse. When the family finally got to the church, it was an hour late. This is *CP Time* at its worst, or best.

5 *Reasons people have used on why they were late for a funeral*

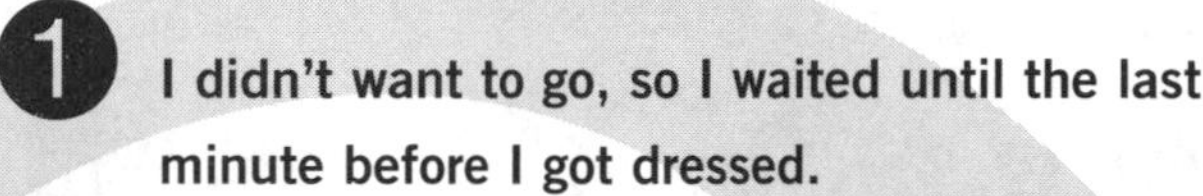

1. I didn't want to go, so I waited until the last minute before I got dressed.
2. I didn't like the mother of the deceased, so I just took my time getting to the funeral home.
3. I got lost, and I didn't stop to ask anyone where the church was.
4. When I got to the church, I had to use the bathroom really bad. By the time I was finished the pastor had started the sermon.
5. I didn't have anything to wear, so it took some time to find something.

We all have heard that saying: "You will be late for your own funeral."

"Here comes the bride..." And she's late as usual.

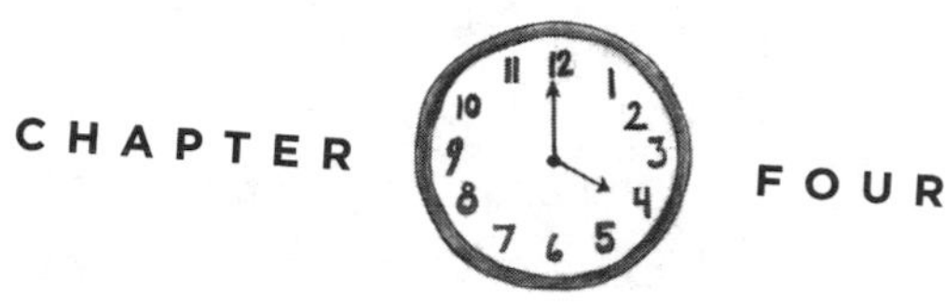

CP TIME AT WEDDINGS

Mr. and Mrs. John Davis III request the honor of your presence at the marriage of their daughter...

The wedding invitation announcing that there will be a happy celebration of two families coming together.

CP TIME AND WEDDINGS DO NOT MIX.

I was experiencing "cold feet" prior to my wedding. I had planned to dress at home since the church was less than an hour away. Everyone had already left for the church; the limousine driver was scheduled to pick me up at 3:50 p.m., and have me at the church by 4 p.m. As scheduled, the driver rang the bell at 3:50 p.m.; I didn't answer the door. The driver went to the church to see if I was already there.

I received a phone call from the wedding coordinator asking where

I was. I said, "I'm waiting for the driver to come." The driver was sent back to the house to pick me up. When he rang the doorbell again, I didn't answer. He returned to the church again without me.

I then received a phone call from my mother asking what was going on. I told her, I was waiting for the driver. She said she was going to send him back and to listen for the car horn. A few minutes later, I heard the car horn, but didn't react. Then I heard the doorbell, and didn't answer it. Shortly thereafter, I recognized my mom's footsteps climbing the stairs. I fell to the floor as though I was looking for something.

When she spotted me, she said, "Fool, what are you doing?"

As I looked up, in full wedding attire, from my hands and knees, I said, the unthinkable: "I'm looking for my contact lens!" She said, "Get up, fool, you don't wear no damn contact lens."

Well, we made it to church fifteen minutes after the wedding was supposed to start.

I DO, EVENTUALLY

I reside in Central Texas, about two and a half hours south of Dallas. Before I married my husband, I hung out with a lot of my Nigerian friends. I was invited to a wedding in Dallas for one of these pals of mine.

I arrived at the wedding hall about twenty minutes early. The sun was shining bright. My clothes were fresh and so was I. Boy, was I on the wrong time. The wedding party didn't show up until thirty minutes after the wedding was supposed to start. Then they had to get dressed. The wedding started an hour and a half late.

Yes, I actually stayed waiting. I drove two and a half hours for a wedding and I intended to see someone get married. By the time they said, "I do," I was pooped. Gave her a kiss on the cheek and got the hell out of there.

WHERE IS THE BRIDE??????

Why would the bride, on the most important day of her life, be late for her own wedding?

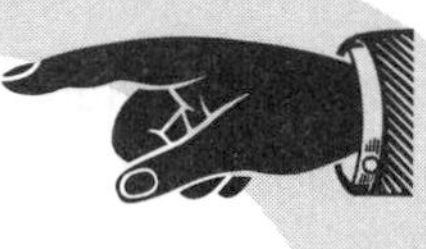

The day I got married was supposed to be a beautiful day. My dad and my uncles planned a day of golf for all of the men in the wedding party. We all met at the golf course to tee off at 8 a.m. The day was wonderful. I was with my closest friends, my dad, and all of my uncles, and, *the boys*. We played fifteen holes of golf before we got ready for my big day.

The wedding was scheduled to start at 6 p.m. My best man was responsible for making sure that we were all on schedule. We rented a hotel suite at the Marriott so that we could prepare for the wedding in comfort. At 11 a.m., all of the groomsmen had their hair cut, beards trimmed, and were receiving some type of necessary grooming. At noon, we had lunch, from 1 to 3 p.m. we relaxed. Some of the brothers took a nap, some played pool in the hotel bar, and some of us watched a movie on the suite's big screen. All the while, my best man kept us on schedule.

He gave strict orders that all of the groomsmen had to be back in the suite, showered and dressed by 5 p.m. and we were. At 5:15 p.m. the limos arrived to pick us up and take us to the church. At 5:30 p.m. all of us were in the church office ready to take our place. We were prepared and ready for the wedding like soldiers ready for war.

We arrived at the church thirty minutes early and ready to get started. By this point, every pew in the church was already full. After the pastor and I had our talk, I greeted my mom and dad. They wished me a life full of love and happiness, and took their place in the church. Next, my best man and I heard the organist playing and the pastor told me that it was time for us to go out and prepare to receive my beautiful bride.

The pastor led my best friend and me down the aisle to our place. Standing in front of the church, I looked out and saw over eight-hundred friends and family members who were there to enjoy and celebrate this special day. As the organist played, the bridal party started marching in one by one on the arms of my boys. It brought tears to my eyes. One after the other, the bridesmaids and all of my men marched down and took their place.

I wanted my baby to come out and appear. I wanted to see my future wife, the lady who I would be sharing my life with, the beat of my heart, the love of my life, the reason I lived. I just could not wait to see her in her wedding dress. Then the organist played that song, the wedding march song, "Here Comes the Bride." As the music started, everyone stood up to greet and see the bride. All eyes were turned toward the back door of the church. The organ continued to play the song, but no bride appeared.

I looked at my future mother-in-law with the question in my eyes, *where is she?* She replied with a looked that said, *I don't know.* The organ continued to play and still no bride. I was beginning to feel that maybe I had been stood up. In fact, I bet that there were a lot of people in the church who began to think the same thing.

The organist continued to play and still no bride. In an attempt to alleviate the situation, the pastor said, "Let's pray." As he went into a prayer, my future mother-in-law got up and left the church. I saw her walk out of the side door and at that point I wanted to leave with her. But I stayed there with my eyes closed and my ears not hearing a word the pastor was saying. In my mind, all I was thinking was,

Where in the hell is she?

The organist was still playing that damn song. I was sick of hearing the song and I wanted to yell, "Shut up for crying out loud," but somehow I restrained myself. When the pastor finished the prayer, there was still no bride. It was then that I decided to leave the altar and walk to the back of the church to the room where she was supposed to be. When I got there, all I found was her mother talking on the phone.

I asked her what was going on. She replied, "It's Jenna. She is still at the house and she is getting her nails done." Apparently, she broke a nail and wanted to get it fixed before she got dressed. My mother-in-law told me not to worry about it and that my bride would be at the church any minute. This was *CP Time* at its worst.

Here are a few other excuses that I've heard from people in regard to why they were late for a wedding:

A MOTHER'S STORY

I was on my way to my daughter's wedding and I needed to stop at a store to get some gum. I couldn't find a parking space close enough to the front door, so I drove around the parking lot a few times until someone pulled out of a parking space closer to the store entrance.

By the time I parked the car, I was already thirty minutes late to the wedding, which was scheduled to start at 2 p.m. It was now 2:30 p.m. I was tempted to call and tell the people at the church that I would be late, but I didn't. I thought to myself: **I'm the mother of the bride; they will wait on me.**

I finally made it to the church at 3 p.m. and when I walked in, the wedding had already started. Instead of taking my place on the front pew, I ended up sitting in the back of the church. I felt so bad, but I knew my daughter would understand.

A GROOM'S STORY

I promised my fiancée that I would be on time for our wedding. I had a problem being on time, and my fiancée had told me that I'd better not be late for my own wedding. I made several arrangements to make sure that I would keep my promise. I started by asking her to call me on the morning of the big day. I even asked my brother to call me at a certain time to make sure that I would wake up. I set all of my clocks in my house. My cell phone clock and my television were set to automatically come on at 7 a.m. I told her not to worry and that I would be at the courthouse on time.

The big day came and all of the clocks went off as I set them. I got up, took a shower, spoke to my baby and told her that I was on time. No *CP Time* for me today. I got dressed, pulled my suitcase to the car, locked up the house and started my route to the courthouse. We planned to go straight to the airport after leaving the courthouse so I wanted to make sure that everything was taken care of when we left.

While driving to the courthouse, I noticed that I was low on gas so I decided to stop at a station to fill the car up. So far, I was ahead of schedule. I figured stopping for gas was not going to make me late so I got off at the next exit and pulled into a gas station.

When I got to the station there was a line at the cashier's window, but I decided to wait. I still had plenty of time before I had to be at the courthouse. I called my fiancée and told her that I had stopped for gas, but I was only about ten minutes away. She sounded a little worried, but I calmed her down. Well, right when I was next to pay for my gas, the cashier's shift changed. As it turns out, this process meant that they had to shut down the window so that the gas station staff could change shifts.

I looked at my watch and decided that I should find another station. I knew of a station that was closer to downtown, and it would also put me closer to the courthouse. I decided to get out of line, get back into my car and head toward the other station. When I got to that station, they were closed due to a problem with the computers. Now I was beginning to feel the pressure of getting to the courthouse on time. I needed some gas. How could such a menial task as getting gas turn out to be a catastrophe?

This situation presented two options: I could either try to make it the courthouse with what I had and possibly run out of gas on the way there, or I could try one more station. I chose the latter and tried another station just a few miles away. When I got to that station, there was a line in front of all the pumps, so I had to wait until a pump was free. At this point, I only had ten minutes to get to the courthouse where I would still have to find parking and get to the judge's chambers. *I can make it, I know I can make it,* is what I kept telling myself.

After a while, I finally got some gas. I jumped back in my car, put my foot to the metal and headed downtown toward the courthouse. When I got downtown, I couldn't find a parking space anywhere. The lots were all full, and at that time I was five minutes late. I tried to call my girlfriend but my cell phone battery was dead. I began to feel the pressure that I had tactically planned to avoid.

When I found a parking space, it was about five blocks away from the courthouse. When I finally got to the room where my fiancée, family and friends were waiting on me, it was over an hour past the time we were scheduled to say our vows. Everybody was looking at me with the look of, *Why are you late?* I had promised them that I would not be on *CP Time* that day and there I was, over an hour late to my own wedding. No one wanted to hear the reasons why I was late. I knew it just as much as them that I was always on *CP Time* and that would probably never change.

Other reasons I've heard from people when asked if they had been late for a wedding

1. I forgot the ring and had to go back home to get it, which made me late.
2. I tore my stocking and needed to stop at the store to pick up a new pair, which made me late.
3. My mother-in-law pissed me off so I didn't want to see her at my wedding. I ended up being late trying to get over her.
4. My dog got sick and I stepped in his poop on my way out the house. I was late because I had to clean my shoes off..
5. The car broke down on the way to the church, so we had to wait on a tow truck to come and tow the car.

6 **I wanted to get married first, so I took my time getting to the wedding. I did not want to see my friend marry before me, I was not engaged yet. I put off going to her wedding as long as I could, I was late.**

7 **I hated the groom.**

8 **I hated the bride.**

9 **I lost the invitation to the wedding.**

"Hello, I'm calling in sick..."

THE NUMBER ONE REASON **why people lose their jobs is being late**. In new employment orientation, employees are told the company's policy of being late, and many companies make new employees sign statements that they have received the company guide that explains the tardiness policy. My best friend, a human resources director, shared with me that his company, a social service agency on the south side of Chicago, has three-hundred employees (99% African American). According to my friend, the number one reason that he has to terminate employees is due to them being late. The company's handbook clearly states: "Dependability, attendance, punctuality, and a commitment to do a good job are essential at all times. Excessive occurrences of absenteeism severely affect the functioning of programs. Disciplinary action may include oral, written, suspension or termination."

The one story that really explains *CP Time* on the job better than any of the stories I received is this one:

I work for a major delivery company in the Human Resources department. I've been working for the company for almost one year. I love my job, I love the people I work with, and I love the opportunities that my company offers.

I am on the fast track to success. I have already picked out my new car...the new Honda EXL, dark blue with tan interior. I have picked out my new apartment. I am currently living with my mother, but those days are numbered. As soon as I cross the one-year mark, I will have made it past the one-year probationary period and I'm in like cement. Two more weeks to go and I get my name on the door. And life will be wonderful. I can exhale.

Over the past eleven months and two weeks, I have made sure that I was never late. I'm not late from coming off my breaks, I'm not late after lunch, I've never been late for a meeting, and I've never been late for any company function. I've seen too many of my people get fired for being late. I read somewhere that the number one reason that African Americans lose their jobs is because of being late. I'm not going to be in that number. I'm not going to let *CP Time* mess up my dreams for total independence. *CP Time* is a four-letter word to me, and I will not let it get in my way. But, *CP Time* has a way to come after you, and trip you up if you let your guards down.

Let me share my *CP Time* story:

I decided that I would stop and pick up a box of donuts for the office. I wanted to make a good impression on my boss, and my boss's boss was going to be at the office today, and I wanted to win some points with both of them. Fresh baked donuts would do the trick. I go to my favorite donut bakery and was there five minutes before they open. They always open up at 6 a.m. sharp and I wanted to get my hands on some of the donuts that would be right out the oven. I wanted the ones that were still hot to the touch.

I pulled into the bakery parking lot and I noticed that there were a few people standing at the door waiting for the store to open. I easily found a place to park, and jumped out my car. I wanted to be one of the first five in the door and I was number four. I spoke to the lady in front of me, and pulled out my wallet to make sure I had some cash. I wanted to make sure that there were no potential hold-ups.

It was now 6 a.m. sharp and the door would be swinging open. Everybody was looking at their watches to make sure that it was six a.m. sharp, including me. At 6:10 a.m. we were still standing in line, and the door had not been unlocked. A brother who was number one in line, was looking real hard in the window, and even knocked. No reply. At 6:25 a.m., there were at least twenty-five people in line behind me. These donuts are so good you wait on them; for me, not this morning. I needed to get in and out and to the office before 7:30 a.m. We are all required to clock in and they only give us a two-minute period before we are considered late. At 6:40 a.m., there was about to be a riot outside of the bakery. No one had opened the doors, no one had stuck their head out the door to tell us it would be a few more minutes, and there was no movement inside. There was no one at the counter, no donuts on the shelves, but the lights were on. By now, everybody was talking and getting upset.

The sister in front of me called the number on her cell phone, no answer. The brother behind me started cussing, talking real loud, saying, "This is why black folk can't keep a business, and that is why I shop where *white folk* live and with *white folk*. If this were a white business, they would have been open on time, or at least have told us there was a problem, and serve up hot coffee for the inconvenience. Not black folk, we are always, on *CP Time...*" He went on and on. And everybody agreed with him, which gave him more fuel to *dog out* this business and all black folk.

At 6:46 a.m. I told myself I needed to go. But, I had waited for forty-five minutes; I might as well wait a few more. I was sure they would be opening the doors in a few minutes and I could still make it to the office in plenty of time. At 6:50 a.m., a few people left the line. They angrily got in their cars shaking their heads and cussing out the store as they drove off. The *faithful five* in line, which included me, still stood firm. By now we had all talked and exchanged *CP Time* stories. Everybody was upset because of one reason or another. I told the sister in front of me that I had to leave in the next five minutes so I wouldn't be late for work. She told me, I needed to go, or **I would lose my job waiting on these sorry-ass people.** Now it was 7 a.m., and I had to leave, without the donuts. So, I gave up my VIP place in line and headed to my car. As soon as I got in the car and started it up, they opened the doors. What did I do? By now, the line was all pushing to get in the door, and there was no way I could tell this mob that I was number five in line and had been in line since 6 a.m. Who cared? So I left. Pissed off, no donuts and running late. The first time in eleven months and two weeks that I was running late, cutting it close.

As I headed to my place of employment, everything you could imagine got in my way. I got stopped at every red light. I got in the wrong lane, the lane with all the slowest drivers. I got stopped because someone wanted to turn and no one would let them turn, which made me and everybody behind me have to stop and wait. Then I had to take a detour because this morning the city was working on the streets, patching potholes, of all the mornings.

Well, now it was 7:30 a.m. and I was trying to find a spot in the parking lot of my building. My heart was beating fast, I was sweating and trying to come up with an excuse to tell my boss. I found a spot and started running as fast as I could to the building. Luckily my office was on the first floor, so I could avoid the elevators. I got into the building at 7:32 a.m. I could still make it, I told myself. I ran down the hallway to the clock-in machine. It was now 7:33 a.m. I reached for my time card, and it was not there—*what the ___!!!!* It is now 7:36 a.m.; I'm really late now. And the clock was still ticking. Where was my time card? I went into the office to make sure that everybody saw that I was here even though I was late. When I walked into the office everybody was in the conference room getting ready for a meeting with my boss's boss. I walked in as quietly as I could, and took a seat. I still had not clocked in, but I would explain, and it was clear that everybody saw me.

My boss came in and introduced her boss to all of us, and the meeting started. An hour later, the meeting ended, and I still had not clocked in. After the meeting, my boss asked me to stop by her office and pick up a file that she wanted me to work on—a termination because someone was late twice in one week.

I still had not clocked in. When I finally got back to my office, and started checking where my time card was, I went back to the time machine and right in front of my face was my time card. I guess I had overlooked it in my rush to find it. So, I clocked in. It was now 9 a.m. I would explain; everything should be okay.

Well, later that day, I got an email from my boss asking me to come by before I left for the day. When I got to her office, she was on the phone and motioned for me to have a seat. When she finished her call, she said, "Why were you late this morning?" I explained to her about the donuts, the traffic, and the time card mishap. She told me that because the Human Resource staff was the role model for the entire company, and because the company took pride in having no tardiness and bragged that all of the employees were always on time, she would have to let me go.

WHAT!!!!! Because I tried to get donuts for you so you can impress your boss, I'M FIRED. NO WAY. She told me that if she didn't let me go, then it would not be fair to all the other employees that lost their jobs because of being late. Plus, I had not clocked in until after 9 a.m., which really stood out.

"But, but, but...I tried to explain to you that I was here," I pleaded.

"But were you here by 7:32 a.m.?" she asked.

I wanted to tell her that if the owner of the bakery had been on time, and not on *CP Time*, then I would not have been late. That it was not my fault but the fault of other folk who lived on *CP Time*. But, she wouldn't understand. She was white, and *CP Time* is a black thing that has ruined my life again. Damn.

 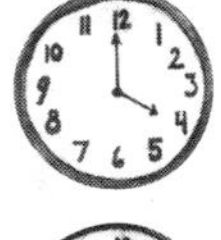

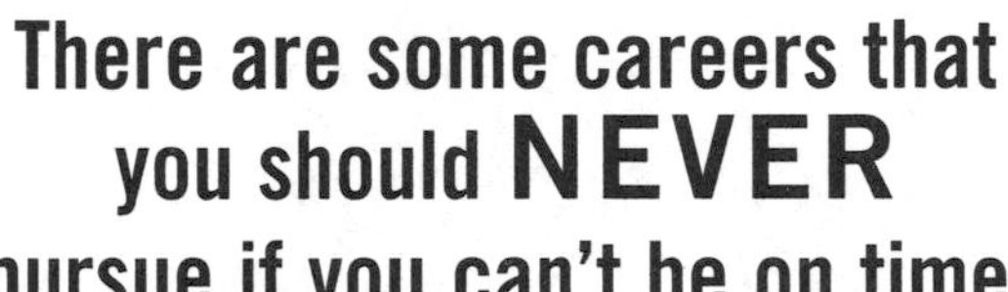

There are some careers that you should NEVER pursue if you can't be on time:

Firefighter (do I need to say more?)

Airline pilot (mechanical/weather delays—OK, human tardiness—not OK)

Military (wars don't wait to start because of CP TIME)

Medical field

Law Enforcement (no one wants a late police officer in case of emergency)

Education (teachers, professors, anyone who is required to teach a class)

TV/Radio (on-air personalities)

Air Traffic control (can't imagine someone showing up late to direct planes)

Emergency response

Wedding planners/coordinators (See Chapter 4)

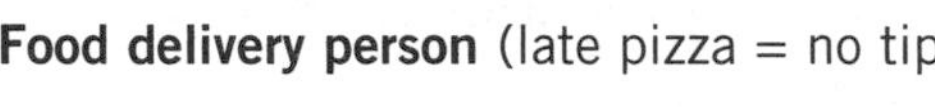

Food delivery person (late pizza = no tip)

Mover

The top 20 reasons that people use when they are late for work!

1. I forgot to set my alarm clock, or my alarm clock didn't work, and I know I set it.
2. Couldn't find one of my shoes.
3. The bus or train was late, but I was at the stop on time.
4. I ran out of gas on the way to work.
5. My child did not want to get up, that made me late.
6. My spouse wanted to have sex before I left for work.
7. I wanted to be late to get fired. I hate this job!
8. I couldn't find anything to wear.
9. I had to get my hair done before I came to work.
10. I was stuck in traffic.
11. The line was long at Starbucks and I wanted a cup of coffee.

12. I wanted to see if I won the contest that was on the radio and they were taking too long to make the announcement, but I was in the parking lot, so I was really here on time.
13. I couldn't find my office, went to the wrong floor.
14. The elevator was broken, so I had to take the stairs.
15. I had to go to the bathroom and that made me late.
16. My dog messed up my clothes, so I had to pick something else to wear.
17. I thought today was Saturday.
18. I thought today was a holiday.
19. Didn't you get my e-mail that I would be late?
20. I told my supervisor that I would be late; didn't she tell you?

One morning I got into a major fight with my wife, and on my way to work, I drove right past my office. In fact, I drove almost ten minutes before I realized that I had driven past the building. We had fought about a bill, and it really upset me. When I realized that I was about ten minutes from being late, and was already too far past the building to make it back on time, I had to come up with an excuse to give my supervisor for being on *CP Time*.

It's funny, I am the one always talking about the other black employees who are always late. Well, this morning, as I sat in traffic watching the time go by, making me even more late, I decided to just call off work. When I called the office to let my boss know that I wouldn't be coming in, she told me that I was needed in the office today and if I didn't get to the office within the next five minutes she would have to dock my pay for the day. Dock my pay, I can't afford to have my pay docked, which was the reason I was late, because of money. Well, **I ended up losing a day of pay, and almost my job, because I arrived to my office on CP Time.**

My co-worker and I decided to ride together one morning to work. On the way, she decided that she needed to make a stop to get her hair edged up. She told me that her "kitchen" was in bad shape and she just wanted to get it edged up before we got to the office. Well, I'm thinking we have time, because normally the boss doesn't arrive until 8 a.m., and it was almost 7:30 a.m. when she picked me up.

Well, to make a long story short, we get to the salon, and instead of leaving because the stylist was not there, we decided to wait. At 7:50 a.m., the stylist was still not there, so my girlfriend decided to call the boss and leave a message on her phone that her son was not feeling good, so we would be late by a few minutes. She told her on the voice mail that she wanted to drop her son off at her mother's house, then come to work, and that I was with her.

As we waited on the stylist to show up (and she was on *CP Time*), our boss walks into the salon and sees us sitting there. Well, we both felt like crawling out the back door, but only thing we could do was sit there. When our boss sees us and ask us why we are not at work, my girlfriend said that she had to stop in to pick up something for her mother before she dropped off her son. Our boss asked her where her son was, and she said her son was sleep in the backseat. Our boss looked at both of us, knowing that we were lying. Well, my girlfriend grabbed me, and we ran out the shop. We made it to work over forty-five minutes late.

The funniest *CP Time* story I have ever heard was from a woman at the office who seemed to be late every other Friday. Not excessively late, but late, say fifteen minutes or so. She never offered an explanation and figured if her boss didn't say anything, she wouldn't say anything.

One day the boss was having a hard morning, in walks this woman, on a Friday about fifteen minutes late. The boss starts berating the woman, yelling and questioning her dedication. Ten minutes into this (in front of everybody) the boss yells at the woman and demands an explanation as to why she is late every other Friday.

The woman yells back, "Because that when my man wants me to give him a blow job, and after I have finished him off, that's when he turns around and gives me the best sex which keeps me from going off up in this mother *@$$#*%*!" I broke out laughing at her admission and as the union representative; I also had to defend her job, which I did successfully.

I worked at a hotel in a major city. The chef, wait staff and banquet manager would always start preparing the meals for black groups one hour after the meal was to start because they understood that some black organizations, especially church groups, never start on time and that for them *CP Time* meant put the meal in the oven one hour after the event is scheduled to start, and be ready to serve the meal two hours later.

I remember one major black event was scheduled to start at 7 p.m. with the opening prayer, dinner at 7:15 p.m. But because of the prayer lasting twenty minutes, and then the hostess talking about how powerful the prayer was, and how everybody needed to be thankful for being alive and at the event, and on and on and on...the meal wasn't served until 8 p.m.

The kitchen staff was trying to keep the already plated meals hot, and was in a panic. When the meal was finally served, everybody complained that the food was cold and started sending the plates back to the kitchen...it was a mess... LOL

The chef and cooks could have killed everyone in the room. The audience actually complained that they would never come back to the hotel, because the food was cold...THE NERVE. Some businesses understand *CP Time* and they have built in to their schedule that if it is a black group, that means, *it will start late.*

CP TIME AND SCHOOL

Being a *CP TIME* student can cost you. At an historically black university a friend who is a professor makes the students who take his class sign the below statement so they will understand that *CP Time* does not work in his class.

> *Being on CP Time will impact your grades and have a direct impact on when and if you graduate.*
>
> ***Attendance:***
>
> *Attendance is required. The final grade-average will be penalized due to excessive ABSENCES and TARDIES: After the second unexcused absence, the final grade-average will be lowered one grade (for example, from A- to B+) for every unexcused absence. Seminar participants arriving more than ten minutes late will be marked absent. The seminar participation grade will be penalized due to excessive (unexcused) late arrivals and early departures.*

Too many young brothers and sisters are fired for being late to work. Why? Do they really care? Why are they not taught the importance of being on time and how it can impact future growth and success?

Humppph...some nerve!

CHAPTER SIX
CP TIME AND CHURCH

When God's Time Is Always On Time!

MY DAD USED TO ALWAYS SAY that **God is always on time!** I grew up hearing at church services, "You can't rush God. God will always show up and show out, God is a quick and fast redeemer, God made the heavens and the earth in seven days."

I have heard many church members stand up during testimony, and tell the church how God showed up right when a major problem was about to happen, or how God showed up, on time, when a child was in an accident, or how God is never late, and will be there before you can hurt yourself, or would expeditiously send the fastest angel to protect you...on time!

I have to admit that I have been upset with God, when I wanted that new BMW right now! Not tomorrow! I wanted God to not be late, but give me what I wanted right now. But, God would always show up on *CP Time*...late! I would be so angry. I would get what I asked for, but because I didn't get it when I wanted it, I had the nerve to be upset with God. Little did I know, at the moment, that what I asked for was not on *CP Time*, but the right time – *God's Time.*

Over the course of my life, I would experience many, many of what I thought was God's *CP Time* behavior, but to my advantage was *God's Time*, not *CP Time*, but the *PERFECT TIME*! God is taking care of *God's People.*

I know personally that God's Perfect Time, saved my life, saved me from hurt, harm, and danger, and this perfect timing happened when I didn't know it was happening. When the car in front of me took too long to make that left-hand turn, which meant I had to wait on the red light. But, right when I stopped for the light, there was a car that went speeding through the yellow light, which if I had taken, would have caused me to be in a major accident. Or when I missed my plane, and that plane was diverted to another city because of engine problems, because a taxi was moving too slow. If I had not been on *CP Time*, I would have ended up on that plane which would have made me late for my destination anyway...

I also laugh at people who drive real fast. They speed by you, and look at you as if you were moving as slow as a snail. They would peel rubber trying to get around you, and you would always catch up with them at the light. As fast as they were going, they still didn't get anywhere.

I am not the most patient person that you will meet. My daughter, Ebony, tells me all the time that I need to get some patience and people are not going to move any faster just because I want them to. My best friend always is telling me that I need to learn how to slow down and enjoy life, that I am too hyper, and I rush too damn much. He tells me what will happen will happen, with or without you, so you might as well just take your time.

I hate *CP Time*! It drives me crazy, and maybe that's why I have no patience. I always want to be where I need to be, and I hate waiting on others who are close to being on *CP Time* for an event, affair, dinner, or anything. I start to huff and puff and walk around in circles, and ask over and over again, "Are you ready, can we go, do you know what time it is, or we are going to be LATE! And the person that I am waiting on still takes his or her time, and is not ready until they are ready. Screw my impatience. I am the one with the issue, and I am the one that is tripping. They are cool and calm. I am a wreck and my nerves are shot. As I get older, I am learning to just chill out. That God really has all of this under control, and there is nothing I can do to alter the situation. This doesn't mean I live on *CP Time*, but I know that when I get there, which is always before the appointed time, it is the right time, *God's Perfect Time*!

I have read many stories of people who survived major events in our history because they were late because of being delayed because of some sick child, or slow-moving mode of transportation, or they were not feeling good when they woke up, or the alarm clock didn't go off on time, or something that just slowed them down that made them run on *CP Time*. This is not just African Americans, but **all people.** I can remember reading several stories from survivors of 9/11 who didn't show up for work on time that dreadful horrible day because they were running late. I remember one story about a lady who said that when she woke up that morning her mother called her and wanted to talk about a problem she was having with her bathroom sink. The sink had been dripping all night, and had kept her up. The mother wanted her daughter to call the building manager for her before she left her apartment to catch the train to the World Trade Center. But, the lady kept trying to tell her mother that she had to get to the train station, or she would miss her train that would get her to work, on the ninety-ninth floor of the North Tower by 8:50 a.m.

This particular morning the mother was upset and wanted her daughter to deal with this problem. The lady thought it was such a small issue that could wait until she got to her office. She would call the building management office as soon as they opened, and get them to take care of the problem. But her mother did not want to hear that; she wanted her to call the before-hours emergency number right then, before she left to catch the train. Well, she ended up missing her train that would have put her at her desk at 9 a.m., which was right before the United Airline Flight 175 hit the South Tower. Everyone she worked with who was at work that morning was killed. In fact, the window that the plane hit was on the side of the building where her office was located. She was saved because she missed her train, *CP Time*.

And there are hundreds of stories of men and women, boys and girls who were saved because they were late to where they were scheduled to be, before the disaster struck.

In my research I read that there were a hundred people who missed boarding the Titanic because they were late getting to the dock before it set sail.

There were a hundred people who missed boarding the Titanic because they were late getting to the dock before it set sail.

I once heard a joke that the reason there were no "colored" people killed on that ship, was they all missed the departure time because they were on *CP Time*.

So we have to ask ourselves if *CP Time* is always a bad thing, or is it a good thing because it has saved lives?

I took piano lessons as a child. I was very good and one of my teacher's favorite students. It was fall and a recital was scheduled for a Saturday afternoon. I can't recall why I was late arriving for my piano lessons. My father is the type who always arrives early if not right on time, always, but not this day. On this day, he overslept, which made me late for this very important day.

When we arrived at the church for the event, everyone was already seated, and one of my friends was playing her piece. According to the program, I was next up. So I guess I wasn't late. But, when I took my seat, and waited for my turn to play, the teacher told me that I would not be playing at the recital, because I was not on time. That all the students were supposed to be at the church thirty minutes before the recital started to practice their songs. I sat there upfront with all of my fellow students and felt really bad.

My dad, who was sitting way in the back of the room, didn't know that I was not going to be playing because we had arrived on *CP Time*. When it was over, he came rushing to the front asking the teacher and me, why didn't I play. My teacher told my father, "The next time, get your daughter here on time...I don't run my recital on *CP Time.*" From that day to this day, I am always on time. That was a lesson that has stuck with me for over thirty years.

Tick-tock, tick-tock, tick-tock...

CHAPTER SEVEN

CP Time and Family

ONE REASON THAT I AM ALWAYS LATE is that I am always talking on my cell phone while I'm getting dressed. I will talk to my mother, my girl and anyone that calls. When I'm on the phone, I normally will sit down and just talk. I won't get dressed, or even cut the conversation short, knowing that I am running late.

One time, my dad called to ask me about his laptop. He couldn't get it to re-boot or something. I was on my way out of the door to pick up my girlfriend who was waiting on me, and told me not to be late, or she was going to leave without me. Well, I started talking to my dad, and before I knew it, it was thirty-eight minutes past the time when I was supposed to pick up my girl, and she lived about twenty minutes away.

That means I would have been almost an hour late. Well, she didn't call, and when I got to her house, she was gone, her car was gone and I just went back home. Later that night when I called her, she didn't call me; I asked her why did she leave me. **She hung up the phone, but not before telling me, to never call her again.** So, I lost another girlfriend because of my *CP Time* behavior.

Our family gets together every Thanksgiving, at a designated family member's house for dinner. Ever since I was younger my parents made us late to the point where my family had to tell my parents that dinner started at 1:00 when it really started at 3:00. So my first year of having a car I drove myself to Thanksgiving dinner. I was told to be there by 12:30; I arrived at 12:20.

My parents said they were leaving right behind me. It's about a thirty-minute drive from my house to my cousin's house; three and a half hours after I got there my family still hadn't showed up. I called my mother, father, and younger sister on their cell phones with no answer. I'm getting really worried thinking something happened to them. Being hit by a drunken driver was the one thing that really stuck out in my mind.

Dinner had already started and still no parents, so my cousin and I got in my car and drove the half-hour drive back to my house; come to find out my dad was watching the FOOTBALL GAME! Their excuse: **"We're always late, this year is no different."**

We know that my brother-in-law will be on *CP Time* for all family functions, even if he has to bring something. So, for instance, if Thanksgiving dinner will be served at 5 p.m., we tell him it'll be served at 2 p.m. so that at 5 p.m., he'll be walking through the door with the fried turkey.

I am constantly struggling against the tendency to be late and to procrastinate. I "got it honest." My mom was ALWAYS late when I was growing up. We usually arrived about a half-hour late for religious services every single week.

It was a habit I quickly picked up and even though I was the closest one to my school bus stop in junior high school—I missed the bus one to two times per week. I remember my mom taking a bath—not a shower, but a soak in the tub bath—at 5:40 a.m. when she had to be at work at 6 a.m., and her job was fifteen minutes away. Somehow, she never quite got why that didn't make sense. One day she got up screaming at us that we were making her late for work because our car was parked behind hers. Guess what time it was? You guessed it—around 5:55 a.m.

Did she stand me up?

Have you heard these sayings
or have you even used one or all of them?

Love makes time stand still, when you are in love there is no such thing as time.

Who needs time? I am in love. I don't want this moment to ever end...if I could just freeze this time to live it over and over.

Being with the one you love is like one continuous minute. It's so beautiful that you lose all track of time.

Relationships have been tried because of the impact of being late, *CP Time*. **Dating someone who is chronically late can break a relationship.** In this section, I take a look at how *CP Time* impacts family and friend relationships, love and dating. I would love to know how many marriages have ended because one of the mates being late for romantic getaways.

Many of us will do many things for love. We act like little children when we are in love, and for the most part there is nothing that a new love can do wrong in our eyes. Love sometimes blinds us to the faults of the one we love.

I spoke to a relationship expert who told me that many couples come to him for help because of individuals who are always late: Late for work, which causes them to lose their job, which impacts the family income; late to pick the children up from school. Late for appointments that are important, and even late to bed, which impacts the lovemaking time and causes major problems in the bedroom, and outside of the bedroom. He told me that he informs his clients that consideration of each other's time should be a priority, for each party. That one should not take for granted the precious time, of his, or her mate just because they are married. That they should make sure that they respect their spouse by being on time, and keeping their commitment to be on time for anything that impacts the other person.

When *CP Time* takes over a relationship, things start to get ugly sometimes, and many couples have ended up splitting because of *CP Time*. One story that a friend told me about his relationship was interesting...hear how *CP Time* ended his relationship.

"If she makes me wait for her one more time when we're scheduled for a date, then I am ending the relationship," is what one man told me in Chicago. He shared with me that his girlfriend, Monica, of over six years, has never been on time for anything.

She was late for everything. She didn't think she had a problem with her timing. **In her eyes, it was everybody else that had an issue, not her.** She would be late for important events that I took her to. She would be late for dinner reservations, late for work, late for making love with me, and late for appointments that impacted both of our lives. *CP Time* was her middle name. She had the audacity to show up late to an event and act like she was on time. She had a demeanor that would dare someone to question her about her *lateness.* But this time I was serious. I told her that if she was late for my dad's retirement dinner party, I was going to end the relationship. This dinner was the most important thing to my family and I didn't want to show up late. She reassured me that she would not be late. She even promised my mom that she would be there early to help out.

Before the dinner party started, I called her to see if she wanted me to pick her up or if she wanted to drive. Since she promised my mom that she wanted to help, and I didn't want to get to the house early, we decided that we would meet each other at my parents' house.

When I got to their home, I headed to the kitchen to see my girlfriend. I looked around the kitchen for her, but I didn't see her anywhere. My sisters, who were in the kitchen, came over and hugged me. At the same time, our next-door neighbor, Ms. Jones, was taking the turkey out of the oven. She waved at me and went back to attending to the turkey. I really wanted to see my girlfriend and I thought that perhaps she was downstairs in another room.

My parents had two kitchens, one in the basement where my grandmother baked her famous apple pies. My dad decided he wanted us to be in the pie business, so he turned the basement into a full-production pie-making company. I said my hello's to the other sisters in the kitchen and headed down the stairs to see if my love was talking to someone, or taking a tour of the operation. When I got downstairs, I saw my grandmother taking out some pies. I gave her a hug and a kiss on the cheek. I asked her if Monica was down there. My grandmother said, "No baby, I have not seen her." *OK,* I thought. *I'm not going to get upset.* I ran back upstairs, and asked my sisters in the kitchen had anyone seen Monica. Everyone said in unison, "No."

I then called her from my cell, and when she answered, I asked, "Where are you?"

She replied, "I'm on my way. I just had to take care of some things before I got to the house."

"What things?" I asked, trying to be calm.

In a reassuring tone, she responded, "Don't worry, I'm on my way, and I'll be there in a few minutes."

An hour later, she had not arrived. Everybody was now sitting around the table eating. The toast was over; the exchange of congratulations was complete. The gifts had been opened, and the table had been cleared. I tried my best to remain calm and not show how upset and hurt I was.

My best friend asked me where was Monica? My mother, who knew that Monica's middle name was *CP Time,* didn't say a word, but the look in her eyes said it all. My sister, who hates when people are late, made a smart crack: **"Well, maybe she was kidnapped by some terrorists, and they took her to the Middle East, and that is why she is late."**

That remark caused everyone to laugh, but I didn't see anything funny. Then she walked in. She came over to me, hugged me and said sympathetically, "I'm sorry that I'm late, but I'm here." It was like it was no big deal to her. She spoke to everyone and gave my dad a gift-wrapped box and told him how happy she was for him. It was like she was not late.

I asked her if I could see her outside, and she followed me to the front porch. I was trying to be cool, but as soon as we stepped onto the porch, I looked at her and asked, "What took you so long? You are over ninety minutes late."

She unabashedly proclaimed, "I told you that I had something to do first."

"What was so important that you had to be late to my father's retirement party?" I asked.

She answered, "I had to pick up a gift for your dad. I went to the mall before I got here."

"The mall? You went to the mall. Why didn't you take care of that yesterday or last week!" I exclaimed, screaming at the top of my lungs.

"I got tied up. But don't holler at me. I am here, so what is the big deal?"

She didn't get it. **She really lived her life with the mentality that being late was acceptable.** She is the epitome of living on *CP Time*. The relationship went downhill from there. I no longer wanted to see her. She didn't care enough to be on time for an important date with my family, and her attitude suggested that she didn't do anything wrong. I was not trying to change her at thirty-two years old. She would always be late, and that was not how I wanted to live my life.

My *CP Time* excuse for always being late is because whenever I'm on time, everybody else is late and then I have to end up waiting on them, and I hate to wait. One example of this is whenever I was to be picked up by my boyfriend, I would not get dressed, take a shower, or do anything according to the time that he said he would be there. I would wait at least one hour before I would start getting dressed; this would really make both of us on *CP Time*. And he had the nerve to get angry at me and blame me for missing the previews at the movie because he was late, and I made him wait.

I was late for a very important dinner party because I decided I wanted to see the last minute of the NBA all-star game. The game was almost over, but I was not dressed yet. My girlfriend and her parents were already at the restaurant. She had not called me yet, assuming I was on my way. I didn't stop watching the game, until it was over. I sat there and watched the ending. I now was about twenty minutes late for the dinner.

I finally received a call from my girl asking me where I was. I told her that I was stuck in traffic, but was almost to the restaurant, when in fact, I was still at home, in my underwear, watching the last minutes of the game. I didn't get to the restaurant until almost forty-five minutes late.

The first thing, her father said to me was "Young man, black people will never get anywhere if they are always on *CP Time.*" Learn to keep your appointment on time." Needless to say, my girl didn't speak to me for a week. **I don't know why she was tripping; I did show up, and I was looking good, too.**

YOU'RE late!... No, YOU'RE late!

CHAPTER 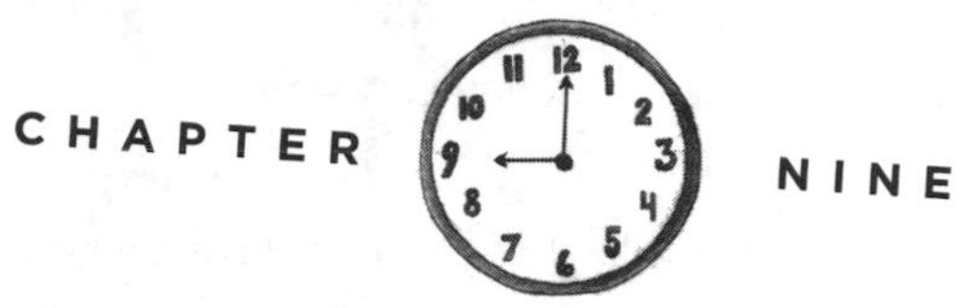 NINE

CP TIME—IS IT JUST A BLACK THING?

"Different cultures communicate differently. Every culture has its own communication style, and its perception of time; the question is how do you release your perception of time, to your world." *Shernaz*

I WANTED TO KNOW if black people are the only ethnic group who are always late. **Is being late a problem for other ethnic groups?** I did my homework and asked some other non-African Americans if being late was a problem in their cultures, and if so, what are those people called?

My buddy who is French told me that in his country people are not late, they are always on time.

My friend who is from Ghana told me that in Africa when people are late it is called "African Time," which means the same thing as *CP Time*.

A man from Thailand didn't have a term for people who are late in his country.

Many people from other countries who move live in America don't understand *CP Time* and many have their own concept of time.

[
A contribution from an African:

"Ancient African people, also contained their value of time, not based on the European concept, the difference between the Western mechanical and African emotional time consciousness, is a highly instructive one. As a black man you find yourself computing time with events for further understanding of the time, you are more than likely experiencing the original African concept conflicting with the Western concept."
]

Another man from Zimbabwe said,

"If the sun is still up,

African Time as explained to me from the perspective of a man from the country of Nigeria:

"What man is a slave to time? We are not slaves to time. It comes naturally that human nature has something inborn that perceives time. We followed the sun. Human beings existed before the clock. What man is slave to time because they made it in order, to prove and enforce it, and stress the concept that they have to obey the law of time, so because the concept was brought to us over there (Africa) due to cultural contact we now follow the clock. It is not our culture, in the olden days we did not have the concept. When they (white men) came and scrambled for Africa, Africans did not have a clock; it was brought by the white man, in order to teach people the concept of time they had to be taught to be a slave to it. People used to tell time with the sun."

Another story I've heard from a young woman (part African and part American):

On her sixteenth birthday she was taking her time preparing to go out with her father, (who is African) and her sister. She was late getting ready, on *African Time*, as lateness is called in some parts of Africa. Her father (from Ghana) told her he needed to teach her a lesson; she was left at home while her sister and father went out on her birthday.

you are not late."

I really wanted to know what White people think about *CP Time*. I asked my good friend Kim, who is white and married to a black minister, if she had ever been impacted by *CP Time*, and she shared this story with me:

When I was twenty-three I decided that I wanted to start a career path in the corrections field. I am not sure now if it was just some type of rebellion against my own background or if it was just some interest of the unknown. At any rate, for the first time in my life, I found myself the minority. That is putting it mildly. I was the only white correctional officer and the only female at the time working with the inmates.

I guess you could say that it was somewhat like being thrown into the lion's den.

My parents had sent me to a private high school and then a small Methodist college to "shelter" me from such environments, but I was determined to see the other side. What led people to come to prison? Where had their lives taken such a turn? Well, after about five minutes into my new job, that was the least of my concerns.

It wasn't that I was racist. I mean after all, there was a black guy in my high school, I think he is a doctor now, but I liked him...just as I knew that I would like my co-workers.

To make a long story short, I did like my black, male co-workers and I quickly learned that we are all the same when it comes to humanity, but our cultures quickly collided.

So many things amazed me...I had never seen people eat a chicken leg and thigh, still with the bone in it, between two pieces of loaf bread, and end up with just a clean bone!!! I would sit in amazement and just stare at this feat. I told all of my friends and family and even tried it myself once, to no avail.

Oh, there were many differences, some funny, some strange, but all delightful just the same. That is, until "the party."

My husband I decided to have a get-together of our friends and my new co-workers. We even had a deejay, something that white people rarely splurge on. Up until that day I had never really thought about our parties. They were never planned or well thought out. We just got friends together, maybe grilled burgers if we had the money at the time, and just drank beer, laughed, and talked. I thought that black people did that, too. But I soon learned that a party means a "party." Good food, good alcohol, nice clothes, etc.

Well, we geared up for our party at 7 p.m. All of our old friends arrived in their Levi's and T-shirts, an occasional polo would be in the crowd...the music blared and I had even purchased party platters of raw vegetables and fruit. I was quite proud of my unusual spread! We danced the night away and as the trashcan filled with empty beer cans the clock clearly reflected 10 p.m. I hid my disappointment from my husband. I was a little embarrassed too that none of my new friends had shown up or even called to make up some lame excuse for not coming. The deejay disassembled, my friends all left, their bellies full of raw broccoli, cauliflower and cheap domestic beer. My eyes stung with tears as I placed the leftovers in the fridge, put on my pajamas and followed my husband to bed. At 11:30 p.m. we heard the doorbell ring. It frightened me at first, thinking that surely someone was dead for our doorbell to ring at such an hour. I put on my robe and stood nervously behind my husband as he opened the door.

Imagine our surprise as we saw eight co-workers standing on the front porch in their Sunday best, holding bottles of Crown Royal and Hennessy. "Why didn't you tell us you cancelled the party?" they all asked. Needless to say, we all got a good laugh as we sat around doing shots, my husband and I in our pajamas, as we learned about the true meaning of *CP Time*.

Stories from white people who don't understand *CP Time* behavior:

STORY #1 THE WEDDING

My wedding was my first lesson about *CP Time.* My name is Mary. I am forty-seven years old. I married a wonderful man who I love with all of my heart. I am white, and he is black. We met at a church conference. His church was holding a couples retreat at the hotel where I worked. He was one of the few single men at the retreat. He was responsible for logistics for the event. When I first saw Tim, it was love at first sight.

I had never dated a black man, so I was a little nervous and didn't know what to say or do. So, I just tried to spend as much time as I could in the room where he and the planning committee were working. The planning committee had checked into the hotel two days prior to the retreat, and I would bring a pot of coffee to the working committee always making sure that Tim received special attention from me.

We began flirting with each other and talked for hours, and the rest is history. We exchanged wedding vows six months later, at his church. That is when I got my first *CP Time* experience.

The wedding was scheduled for 3:30 p.m. I was ready, my bridesmaids were all ready, and we were waiting for the organist to begin playing the wedding march, as the cue for the wedding party to start the processional. We heard the soloists sing their songs, and we heard the choir (yes, we had a full choir) sing their song. I was nervous and ready to walk out, and down the aisle to marry the love of my life. We waited to hear the organist begin playing, no organ.

The wedding planner came back to tell me that the organist was not at the church yet. She had called, and said she was running late, but would arrive at the church any second.

I looked at Ms. Jones, the wedding planner, and said, "She is not here! What do you mean; she is not here? I don't understand, the wedding has started. How can she not be at the church? **Does she know what time it is?"**

When I said that, one of my bridesmaids, a sister, said to me, "Girl, Sister Pat is always late, she is never on time for anything; that girl lives on *CP Time.*"

CP Time? "What in the hell is *CP Time?"* I asked her.

She started laughing and said, "*CP Time* is when some black folk show up whenever they feel like it, and they don't care whether a wedding, funeral, or their jobs, they cannot be on time for anything."

I learned my first *CP Time* lesson at my wedding. I didn't march down the aisle until thirty-five minutes after I was supposed to. But one thing I noticed, **I was the only person upset; everyone else was cool, and acted like this was normal.** No one said a thing about the wedding starting late, or about Sister Pat playing the organ late. It was never mentioned, so I didn't say a word, either. But, I learned that in the Black community, especially the Black church, that *CP Time* is just part of the culture. *CP Time* is accepted by most, it is a way of life for many.

STORY #2 THE PAINTERS

I hired a black man to paint my house, and they didn't show up until three hours after they were supposed to start the job. I told them to be at the house at 7 a.m. so we could get an early start, and get the job finished. I had stopped at the bakery, and picked up some donuts and coffee for the guys. While waiting for them, I prepared everything for them to get started when they arrived.

The painters had not arrived at 9 a.m. I called the number that I had gotten from the company that provided day labor, and was told that they would be there any minute. At 10 a.m. they showed up and acted like they were on time. They saw me sitting in my truck and waved at me, and started working.

I went over to them and asked why they were so late, and one of them said, **"We are not that late, just got a little side-tracked, but we are here, and ready to work."**

I just scratched my head, and stepped back. I wanted to fire all of them, but I needed to get the job done. I learned later from my good friend who is Black that the guys showed up on *CP Time*.

STORY #3 THE PROM

In high school, I only dated black boys. I love black men. I've have had white people turn their heads when they saw me and my black boyfriends together holding hands. I have been told, by my best friend that I need to *find a nice white boy and leave those black boys alone*. But, I do what I want to do, and I love black men.

In my senior year, my boyfriend and I had made plans to go to the senior prom. The prom started at 7 p.m. I told him to pick me up at

6:30 p.m., so we could get pictures taken and arrive at the hotel at 7 p.m.

Since the prom started at 7 p.m., to me that meant be at the affair at 7 p.m. My boyfriend showed up at my house at 8 p.m. When he finally arrived at my mom's house, I had already taken off my dress, and put on some jeans thinking he had changed his mind, and decided not to take me.

When he showed up in his tux with flowers, I was floored. I asked him why he didn't call me, or let me know that he was going to be arriving late.

He looked at me and said, "The prom started at 7 p.m., but none of the black students will get there until 8 or 9 p.m."

In fact, he said we were going to make a stop before we got to the prom, to see his uncle and aunt, so they could take pictures of us. I got dressed again and left with him. We didn't get to the hotel ballroom until 10 p.m. We were not the only couple walking in at 10 p.m. There were a lot of other couples (all black) arriving at the same time.

This was my first *CP Time* experience and even though I didn't like getting to the prom late, I felt good just being with my boyfriend, and his friends. I fit in with them and being late didn't bother me as much after all. We still had a ball.

STORY #4 EVENTS

You know, I didn't hear the term, CP Time until I was in college. I was in the Magnet program at a football top ten school. The Black Caucus used to say to us when we had events that there was no *CP Time,* if you wanted to make a good impression. I never knew what that meant. Ever since I was born late, my family was always late to Sunday services where the whole row had to hear the "excuse me" or where we had to be split up because there wasn't enough seats in the same area. It was embarrassing.

The director used to say to all of us even though there were more than just *colored folks* there, she'd say, "Why are all of you on *CP Time*? Get here when the schedule says to be here. **She made all of us set our clocks and watches ten minutes fast because the majority of the class, Asian, Hispanic, Colored and Indian, were always late by at least ten minutes.** Some people were left on campus when *CP Time* was an issue. I was at the end of my freshman year before I understood what it meant. After that I've been using it no matter what color the person is. Sometimes it flies out my mouth so fast I forget whom I am talking to at times.

STORY #5 CULTURES

C**P *Time*...I wish there was some way to make it known that times change for time zones, or daylight savings time.** Should there really be a CP 3 p.m., which equates to 3:45 p.m.? I hear that *CP Time* also occurs in other cultures as well. It was interesting to watch the show "Whose Wedding is it Anyway?" on Style Network and hear the couple declare to the wedding planner that Persians are never on time, sometimes even up to five hours late! That was funny.

STORY #6 OPINION

I **am a twenty-one-year-old Caucasian who has a wide range of friends who come from many different backgrounds.** I don't really remember my first time hearing about *CP Time*...I just know what it means and I hear it mentioned way too many times. Maybe it's because I am a bit anal retentive when it comes to being on time but I'm not a fan of *CP Time*. Half the time it's used as an excuse and the other as a joke.

I think having performances, shows, or showing up late for meetings, work...is all extremely unprofessional and just because there is something to call it doesn't make it any better. I now almost assume that every event I go to being held or put on by Colored People is going to start late...and I haven't changed my view on that because every time my point is proved. **I hated typing the "Colored People" part, never mind thinking it...but I didn't make up the term. Also, if I came up with a term like WP Time...white people time...it wouldn't be right.**

How dare they leave without us?

CHAPTER 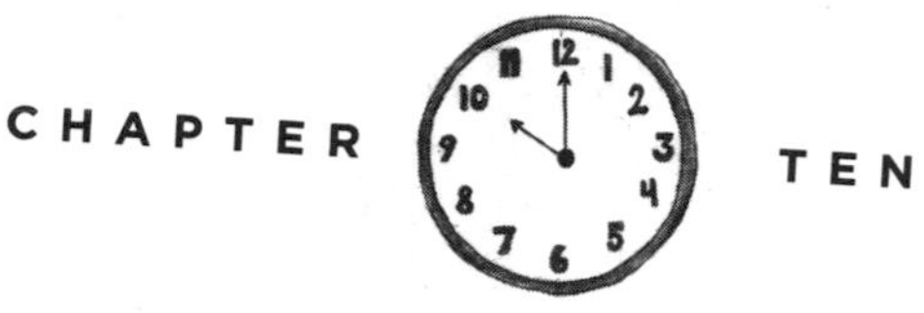 TEN

CP Time In Today's Society Of Fast Technology

I WANT IT NOW. I don't want to wait, need it yesterday, text me, e-mail me, call me on my cell, microwave it, overnight it, UPS, FedEx, DHL...on and on. Being on CP *Time* and using excuses of why you are late is not going to work. I read that there are over nine-hundred million people who have cell phones, so if you are running late, **there is no excuse for not being able to call and let people know that you are late.**

Now, with all of this new high-speed technology, why are people still late and showing up without calling? People who are on *CP Time* who don't call to let others know that they are running late, should stand before a firing squad. There is no excuse not to let someone know you are late.

All you have to do is call. It merely takes one minute to pick up a phone and inform someone of your tardiness. With all of today's technology, you can even send a text message or email if you are going to be late. However, most people just don't think that being late is a big deal.

CHAPTER  ELEVEN

WHAT IF: SCENARIOS

You invite your best friend to attend a party with you weeks in advance, and when you get to their house they are not ready. Do you:

a. Come in and wait patiently, and not complain, no matter how long they take.

b. Help the person get dressed to hurry them along.

c. Get upset and scream at them for not being ready when they knew weeks in advance what time the party started, and walk out and leave them.

d. Just shrug it off, as that's how they are, always late, and deal with it.

e. Go to their bar and start drinking because you are upset.

Correct answer: None of the above—it is not a black and white issue, no pun intended.

When you invite someone to an event, always follow-up with a reminder call the week of the event, and another call the day of the event to remind them of the time. I find some people do not like to say "no, thank you," if they are not interested, and will wait until the last minute to make an excuse. It is easier to say, "I'm running late, go on without me." They knew they didn't want to attend in the first place. Don't pressure someone to attend an event; they might embarrass you by showing up on *CP Time*.

You arrive at a gathering and no one is there yet, and it is one hour after the party was to start. Do you...

a. Keep driving by the location because you don't want to be the first one at the party.
b. Go in and wait.
c. Go back home and wait a few more hours and then go back when you see more cars.
d. Call the host and ask them if anyone is there.
e. Complain that black people can't ever start on time, and go in with a negative attitude.

Correct Answer: None of the above.

If no one wants to be the first one at the party, how will it get started? Go in and get the party started!

Reasons and Excuses (As told by African Americans around the country)

The Worst List

> **"Excuses are tools of incompetence; used to build monuments of nothingness, and those who use them seldom amount to anything!"**
> *Author Unknown*

★ I've heard excuses from people who are late: They fell asleep, were talking on the phone and let time get away from them, they had to put the babies to sleep, had to cook, or got in late from work. They are all good reasons. The only excuse that I give which is true is: I don't drive, I have to ride with someone else.

★ I had on a new outfit and I wanted everyone see me when I entered the club.

★ I had a new boyfriend and I wanted to make sure that everyone saw us enter together.

☆ My ex-girlfriend was going to be at the pool party, and I wanted to be late so she could see me with my new "white" girlfriend.

☆ I wanted everyone to see my new body, so I waited until late to show up so all eyes could be on me. Plus I had on a skimpy little dress that was really revealing.

☆ My breast milk started leaking, in the car, because the seat belt was squeezing me, and ruined my blouse, so I had to go back home and change. I knew I should have put in my pads; it made me late for a job interview.

★ I couldn't get my erection down. So I had to sit in the car until it went down, that made me late.

☆ I had to masturbate before going to work, and that made me late.

☆ I wanted to have sex, so I got on the sex line and it took a long time to meet someone for sex. That made me late for my meeting with my banker. Sex always makes me late.

☆ Ran out of gas, and I knew I was on empty before I left.

☆ No excuse, I just decided I am going to be late; I wanted to make an appearance.

★ The person I was picking up overslept, and lied to me and told me he was ready.

☆ The deceased owed me money, and I wanted to ask his wife when I was going to get my money from her.

☆ My taxi driver wanted to stop at McDonald's to get a cup of coffee.

☆ My taxi driver got lost and blamed me.

☆ I couldn't get out of bed because I wanted more sex from my wife.

☆ I was having sex and didn't want him to stop, even though I knew I was late.

☆ My gas was disconnected and it was too cold to get out of bed.

☆ My electric was turned off and that made me late, because I didn't pay the bill.

☆ I double-booked my appointments and made one wait.

☆ I kept calling the restaurant telling the manager to tell my guest I was on my way, and I wasn't.

☆ My eyes were red, and I was waiting on the Visine to kick in before I left the house.

☆ I had to walk my dog first, and that made me really late.

☆ My dog needed some food, so I had to go to the store and pick up some dog food before I met my boyfriend at the movies.

★ Didn't have any quarters for the meter, so I had to go to several places to get change and no one wanted to give change for a twenty.

☆ Couldn't find an ATM so I had to find one.

☆ Couldn't find a tie without a stain on it to wear to the meeting.

☆ I lost the memo about where the meeting was at and I didn't ask anyone.

☆ I got lost because I thought I knew where I was going.

☆ Lost track of time because I was doing something else.

☆ I forgot to set the clock back when time changed.

☆ Missed the shuttle bus and had to walk to the office.

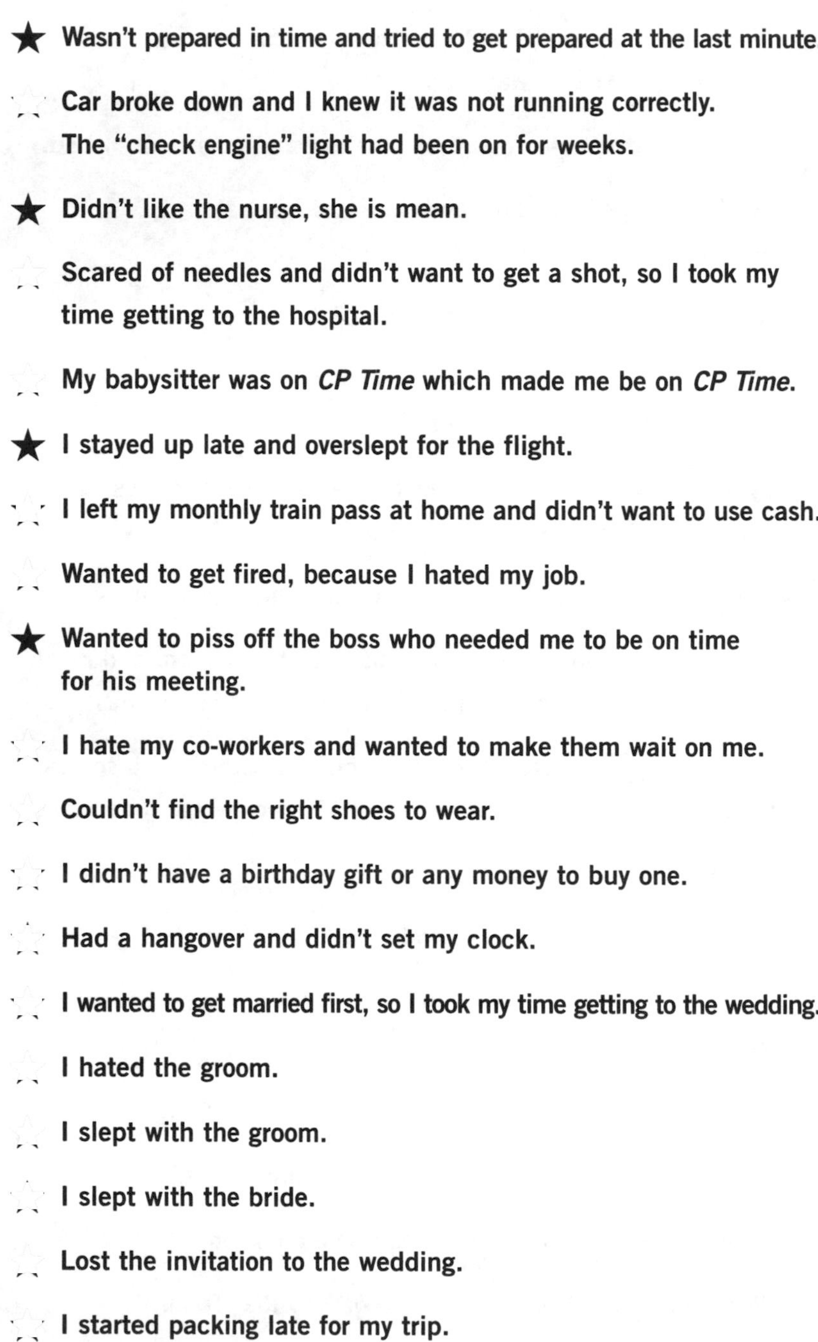

★ Wasn't prepared in time and tried to get prepared at the last minute.

☆ Car broke down and I knew it was not running correctly. The "check engine" light had been on for weeks.

★ Didn't like the nurse, she is mean.

☆ Scared of needles and didn't want to get a shot, so I took my time getting to the hospital.

☆ My babysitter was on *CP Time* which made me be on *CP Time*.

★ I stayed up late and overslept for the flight.

☆ I left my monthly train pass at home and didn't want to use cash.

☆ Wanted to get fired, because I hated my job.

★ Wanted to piss off the boss who needed me to be on time for his meeting.

☆ I hate my co-workers and wanted to make them wait on me.

☆ Couldn't find the right shoes to wear.

☆ I didn't have a birthday gift or any money to buy one.

☆ Had a hangover and didn't set my clock.

☆ I wanted to get married first, so I took my time getting to the wedding.

☆ I hated the groom.

☆ I slept with the groom.

☆ I slept with the bride.

☆ Lost the invitation to the wedding.

☆ I started packing late for my trip.

☆ I couldn't find my air ticket, and I always misplace things, so I should have kept up with it.

★ My mom wanted me to do something for her before I left town.

☆ Was waiting on the mailman to bring me my tax refund check before I left.

☆ I was waiting on the mailman so I could see if my check came.

☆ Didn't buy a ticket to the concert and had to wait in line, even when I told my date I had the tickets.

☆ My date was late, so that made me late.

☆ I saw my ex-boyfriend and I had to hide until he left the restaurant before I went in to meet my date.

☆ My girlfriend was at the bar, and I was meeting another girl, so I made her wait until my girlfriend left the bar before I went in. My date was pissed because she told me don't be late.

☆ I didn't have any condoms so I had to find a drug store that was open to get some, which made me get to my girlfriend's house late.

☆ I was waiting until my favorite song ended that was playing on the radio before I went in to work.

☆ I was listening to the radio to hear if I won the contest or if I was caller number 106.

☆ I forgot to defrost the turkey which made the dinner really late getting started.

☆ I ran out of food and had to go to the store after my guests arrived for dinner.

☆ I work best under pressure, so I always wait until the last minute.

☆ I always get to the party two hours after it starts, anytime before that is too early.

☆ I didn't have any clean underwear so I had to stop at the store and get a pair before I went to church. Then I couldn't find anyplace to put them on without anyone seeing me.

☆ The pastor wanted to pray for me before I left on my trip.
His prayer was too long and I missed my flight.

☆ I am slow getting dressed.

☆ I don't believe in being on time for anything.
It's not my problem if people wait. They will get over it.

☆ I knew the traffic would be bad, but I still waited and left late.

☆ I hate my mother-in-law's cooking and didn't want to be on time for dinner, hoping that everybody would eat everything up first.

☆ I hate my in-laws.

☆ Hated my cousin's son so I didn't want to attend his piano recital.

★ I was broke and lied to my date.

☆ I waited until the last minute to make up my mind.

☆ I couldn't find anyone to tie my tie.

☆ I couldn't find anyone to zip up my dress.

☆ My wife was drunk.

☆ I was drunk.

☆ I couldn't find my Bible.

☆ I stopped to talk to my best friend before going inside.

CHAPTER TWELVE

CP TIME: JUST CALL

If you were running late, why didn't you call???

"I'll get there when I get there" is the attitude of a lot of black folks. **"Don't trip. At least I'm here,"** is what my best friend would tell me when he would show up over an hour late for any event that I invited him to. One time, he was so late to a party that when he got there the party was over, everyone had gone home. He called me from his car asking me what time the party had ended and why I didn't wait on him. The nerve.

My daughter Ebony is always late. She has been late from the day she was born. If you ask her to rush, hurry it up, or "Come on, girl, because you're going to make us late," she will simply tell you, **"Don't rush me."** She just acts like she doesn't hear a word anyone is saying.

One time, I wanted to take her out for dinner and I told her that I made reservations for 7 p.m. sharp. I really made the reservations for

8 p.m., but I wanted us to be there on time so I told her 7 p.m. I did so hoping that she might be ready by 7:30 p.m.

Well, my first-born didn't start getting ready until 7 p.m. and wasn't finished until 8:30 p.m. As it turned out, we ended up not getting to the restaurant until 9 p.m., an entire hour later than the original reservation. I was so upset with my daughter and for some reason she didn't understand why I was upset. She told me that if we had arrived there at 7 p.m., we would have had to wait until 9 p.m. for a table anyway. She knew how restaurants worked and so getting there at 9 p.m. we would be "on time." Theoretically, this was *CP Time* at its best.

As I stated earlier, I feel that a lot of stress can be avoided if a person would just call. Simply tell the person who is waiting that you are running late, and everything will be okay. However, when possible, you should try to be on time. To make another person wait on you is one of the worst things you can do.

Everybody has a story of being the victim of *CP Time*.. One mother told me that her son was two days late being born. He was due on a Wednesday, and didn't come out until Friday. He has been late to everything ever since. **Is *CP Time* inborn in us?**

I emphasize call if you are going to be late, however, sometimes circumstances are embarrassing. How do you call ahead and explain the following circumstances? Sometimes you'd just rather be late than to explain:

- ☆ My gas was disconnected and it was too cold to get out of bed.
- ☆ I didn't have a birthday gift or any money to buy one.
- ☆ I saw my ex-boyfriend and I had to hide until he left the restaurant before I went in to meet my date.
- ☆ I wanted to have sex, so I got on the sex line and it took a long time to meet someone for sex. That made me late for my meeting with my banker. Sex always makes me late.
- ☆ I hadn't bought tickets to the concert and had to wait in line, even when I told my date I had the tickets.
- ☆ I had to masturbate before going to work, and that made me late.
- ☆ I was waiting on the mailman so I could see if my check came.
- ☆ I wanted more sex from my wife.
- ☆ I didn't have clean underwear so I had to stop at the store and get a pair before I went to church. I couldn't find a place to put them on without anyone seeing me.
- ★ I ran out of food and had to go to the grocery store after my guests had arrived for dinner.
- ☆ I didn't have any condoms so I had to find a drug store that was open, which made me late to my girlfriend's house.

- ★ **My girlfriend was at the bar, and I was to meet another girl, so I made her wait until my girlfriend left the bar before I went in. My date was pissed because she told me, "Don't be late."**
- ★ **I was broke; I lied to my date.**
- ★ **I couldn't get my erection down, so I had to sit in the car until it went down; that made me late.**

Take note that all of these excuses begin with the word "I," or "my." Sometimes our self-centered focus makes us late. Perhaps we do not take into account the other parties' interest.

"Opportunity is a door opened for someone prepared."

Utilizing these tips to ensure promptness will make your life less stressful, complicated, and drama-filled. A CP Time mindset is not easy to change; being prompt is a lifestyle change, as is any other change that you want to make. Whether dieting, exercising, or any other change needed to improve your quality of life, it requires a change in how you think.

"It is better to arrive early, and use your wait time productively, than to miss out by arriving late."

Prepare the night before:

Decide at least the day before your event/appointment what to wear, wash and iron your clothes if necessary. You can make yourself late attempting to remove a spot from your clothes, or selecting an alternative outfit, at the last minute.

Do not take phone calls when leaving for appointments, call the person back later; if it is an emergency the other party will find a way to contact you via email, cell phone (which, as a courtesy and proper phone etiquette, should be on vibrate/silent ringer mode during your appointment). We live in an age where it is almost impossible not to be found, unless you are Osama bin Laden.

Map out your route; if you are not familiar with the area, make a "dry run" the day before.

This is one area where a cell phone is definitely okay to use while driving (Use your earpiece!) Call the place of your appointment to walk you through directions while on the phone. **Men, don't let your male ego make you late.** We all know men do not like to ask for directions.

Note:
I have had online map directions, and followed them exactly as written, to find that they were incorrect, therefore, making me late for an important radio interview.

Give yourself plenty of time to arrive on time. Anticipate trains, stopped traffic, construction, weather delays, etc. Do not try to run errands beforehand! Give yourself realistic traveling time, not based on how fast you can drive, or how you can cut off a couple of miles by taking an alternate route. Inevitably those routes will have construction, traffic delays, etc.

Record your appointments in your appointment book, computer calendar with alerts, or your cell phone. Record the date and time immediately when making the appointment. Make it a habit to check your appointments weekly (at the beginning of the week), and daily (at the beginning of the day).

12
11:55
1:15
10:50
2:15
9
3
8:45
4:30
7:45
6
5:30

CP Time: Stories

Fraternity Pledge Line

CP Time almost got me kicked off my Fraternity Pledge Line. When I joined my fraternity, it was the biggest commitment that I had ever made. I was ready for the pledging process, and I was excited about becoming a part of a brotherhood that would be a part of my life forever. When I was on line, being at our assigned location at the designated time was absolutely mandatory—no questions. It was not given a second thought, the possibility that my line brothers could, or would be late; to have to deal with our big brothers, is something that I did not want. We were considered one unit, not nine individuals, so if one *screwed up* we all suffered for it. I made sure that my line brothers were always ready, and we were always where we were supposed to be on time, preferably early.

I was not going to let *CP Time* get me in trouble, however, one night we were supposed to be at a certain location at 4 a.m. I set my alarm to wake me up at 2 a.m. I wanted a two-hour head start to get ready, and get my line brothers up and to the location. At 2 a.m. my alarm went off, but to be honest with you, I really didn't go into a deep sleep. I kind of just lay across the bed fully dressed, so I could be ready. I had seen what happened if you are late, and I didn't want to have the fate of others on my butt.

I jumped up, called my line brothers as planned, and told them, one by one, to get up. When I got to Nick, the last brother on my list, his phone rang and rang but he didn't pick up. I called again, still no answer. I called again, and I called over and over, and still no pick-up. While his phone rang, the only thing I could think of was getting my butt beat, or my big brothers screaming at the top of their voices all kinds of threatening words. I did not want to go through that again, with time quickly going by, this would be a reality. My heart started to beat really fast, and I even felt sweat rolling off my brow. I have to admit, I was getting extremely worried and scared. We were told during the intake process that showing up on *CP Time* was not tolerated by the organization, and was the main reason why a candidate could get kicked off line.

My phone started to ring from the other brothers who wanted to know where I was and what was up with Nick. I told them that someone needed to hurry over to his apartment, and find out if he was dead; that had better be the only reason he was not answering his phone.

Jackie, who lived close to Nick, said he was on his way, and would call me as soon as he got to his apartment. I told him to kick the door down if he had to. I was serious about being on time, and not pissing off the big brothers. When Jackie got to Nick's apartment he called me to let me know that Nick wasn't there, but his roommate told him that he was at his girlfriend's apartment.

I screamed into the phone, **"His girlfriend's house!" What the hell!** I told Jackie to go to Nick's girlfriend's house, which was about five blocks from Nick's place and get his butt, and we would all meet at the location given to us by our big brothers. It was now 3 a.m. I met my other seven line brothers in front of my place, and together dressed in our black sweat suits with black Nikes and skullcaps. We all had a look of fear on our faces. Today could end up being a day of hell, because Nick was not with us and even though we could be on time, it didn't matter; we were one unit.

When Jackie finally tracked Nick down, he couldn't believe that he had overslept. His girlfriend wanted him to give her some time, and he wanted some love from her. He had always been the one brother who would take risks; this proved again that he would put his needs over his line brothers. Jackie let him have a piece of his mind, and dragged him out of her apartment.

We had Nick, but Nick didn't have on his required mandatory outfit. We were required to all dress alike. Nick had on a pair of white sweat pants and a wifebeater. Jackie called me and told me to go to Nick's apartment and get his all black gear and he would meet us at the location. It was now 3:35 a.m. We had twenty minutes to be at the location, and we had to be in position not at 4 a.m., but 3:55 a.m., or we would be considered late and have to deal with the consequences.

Jackie and Nick made it to the location at 3:59 a.m. My other line brothers and I couldn't get into formation because we knew that if we all were not there it didn't matter. We all would be considered late and have to deal with our big brothers. All because Nick wanted to see his girlfriend, and his need to have sex made the rest of us look like we showed up on *CP Time.*

Our big brothers were waiting on us to show up late. They wanted us to be late; they loved the fact that we were late and we all learned a valuable lesson on that day, and to this day, this incident has made me always on time and to never arrive anywhere on *CP Time*.

CP Time is a bad habit that greatly impacted my life that morning. It taught me that some people look at *CP Time* as just being a part of living. But, I will never let anyone make me late again, and I am never on *CP Time*.

THE FASHION SHOW

The Fashion Show did not happen because of my *CP Time* habits. Everybody I knew wanted to get tickets to this year's most popular must-attend fashion show. It was being held at the MLK Performing Arts Center. The tickets were selling for $100 in advance and no tickets where being sold at the door. Either you had tickets, or you didn't. It was the social event of the year. People would spend their last dollar on an outfit and making sure that their automobiles were detailed for the event. It was the one time of the year where if you were anybody you attended this event.

A few local celebrities showed up to walk the "red carpet." The local media were there to take pictures and asked questions about your outfit and the designer. This was not Hollywood, but for my small hometown, it was just as big to our community. The pre-promotion about this event starts six months in advance. The newspapers and radio stations talk about the fashion show as if it were the "second coming of Jesus."

When the tickets went on sale there was a line at the MLK Center's ticket office. I knew the tickets would sell out fast, they do every year. People took off work or would go to work late so they could get in line and purchase a prime ticket. The VIP tickets also were on sale and the sponsoring organization would offer only ten VIP tickets at $250 each, and they were sold on a first-come, first-serve basis. This year, I wanted a VIP ticket. Last year I missed out, because I had to pay a last-minute bill, but this year, I was going to get a VIP ticket. My best friend, Earline, also wanted a VIP ticket.

All the eligible single brothers attended the pre and post VIP reception and VIP's had an opportunity to network with celebrities and other powerful movers and shakers. The VIP tent would be set up outside of the center and last year, when we left the show, I saw all the "beautiful" people going into the tent for a night of dancing and eating great food that was catered by the best restaurant in town. The searchlights would be shining into the sky and limos were parked in front of the VIP tent.

I was determined to be on that list this year. Hell, I am a forty-year-old single sister who is looking for a husband. What better place than at the one event that every single brother in the surrounding area and outside of the community would be attending? **My chances of meeting "Mr. Right" were very, very high. And I was going to be there.** I had purchased my little black dress, a hot pair of Jimmy Choo's six-inch stilettos. Last year I had my breasts lifted so I could show off my "girls" at this event. Yes, I took this event seriously and lived all year, just for this night. My life was not that exciting the rest of the year; in fact my hometown out and out sucked socially. There was no real nightlife so when I had the opportunity to party, I was going to go all out.

I told Earline to meet me at the ticket office at 6:30 a.m. sharp. The doors opened at 7 a.m. I figured if we got there at 6:30 a.m., and found a place to park, we could be the first in line to get one of the ten VIP tickets that were being offered to the "everyday folk" like me, who were not president of a board, or married to a lawyer, doctor, or worked in some other public position, in government or city council. My girl Earline was never late for anything, and I knew my girl would be there before 6:30 a.m. with a cup of Starbucks in her hand waiting on me.

I have had some *CP Time* problems in the past. I lost four jobs for showing up on *CP Time*, and even lost a relationship because the brother was tired of me always making him late for everything.

Earline and I talked the night before and made sure that we were on the same page. We would set our alarm clocks for 5:30 a.m. She would call me, or I would call her, whoever got to the phone first. We would head out of our homes at 6 a.m. sharp to make sure we avoided any traffic jams or any other type of situations that might arise. I lived closer to downtown, but she'd get to the center faster than me. I had to drive on the crowded streets.

We even had a plan B that if something happened to either one of us, that the one who got to the center first would purchase both tickets and get reimbursed later. We had out plan together. The night before, I called Earline and we talked until 3 a.m. about how we wanted our hair done, what color our nails and toes would be, and even which bra and panties we were going to wear under our fabulous outfits. When I told her good night, it was 3:15 a.m. I even double-checked the alarm on my cell, the alarm clock on my nightstand, and the alarm on my TV to make sure that I didn't oversleep. Plus, my girl would be calling me when her eyes opened.

At 5:30 a.m. sharp all of the alarms went off. Earline called me, and we were off to a good start. I jumped up, washed my face, brushed my teeth, and got dressed in a pair of cute hot pink shorts and a T-shirt. I loved wearing fitted T-shirts; my new breasts just looked so good, all firm in T-shirts.

I got in my car and pulled out of the driveway and headed downtown. Everything was in line and our plan was on time. My *CP Time* behavior in the past had caused some major problems in my life. I don't know why I couldn't show up on time for anything, but this morning I was on time and would not be late. I was going to be at the VIP event, and *CP Time* was not going to stop me.

On the way to the arts center, I called my girl and she told me that she was on the highway and was about five exits from the exit to the center. She said for some reason traffic was heavy and there had been an accident, so two of the highway lanes were blocked. But, we were okay on time and we would easily be at the center as planned, to get in line to purchase two of those ten VIP tickets.

When I hung up from her, I decided to stop off at the Starbucks and get a tall cup of bold house coffee. I had plenty of time, and my girl was on her way, so we were covered. I pulled into the parking lot of Starbucks and went in. As usual it was a line. People will wait in line for a cup of Starbucks, including me. There is no other coffee like it and if I don't get a cup in my system, I get a headache and get real evil. I know that I am addicted, but it is a good addiction, to me anyway. As I waited for my turn to place my order, I picked up a copy of *USA Today*. When I got to the counter, and placed my order, the young man said that it would be a minute, that they were changing the filters so I could have a fresh cup of Joe. I paid for my cup, the paper, and a bagel and stepped aside. I got my cup and headed back to my car.

When I got to my car, I noticed that someone had me blocked in, so I had to go back into the store and ask if anyone knew who had me blocked. There was a good-looking brother who apologized for blocking me in, and said he would move. He was fine, and smelled better than the coffee. I stuck out my chest to make sure he saw how full and firm my new breasts looked.

We walked out of Starbucks together and when he got to his car, he smiled at me, and said again he was sorry for blocking me. I told him no problem, and smiled at him to let him know that I was not in that big of a rush, and if he wanted to say anything else to me...it was okay. He picked up my *flirting* with him and asked to buy me a cup of coffee for my inconvenience. He was a fine brother, about six feet tall, dark smooth skin with a perfectly shaped bald head. I had a thing for bald-headed brothers.

I told him that would be nice, but I needed to get downtown. He said, "Just one cup and I promise you that I will not hold you up from getting to your location on time." I called Earline; she didn't pick up, so I assumed that she was already at the ticket office and in line waiting on me.

The brother told me his name, Nate, and that he worked for a local manufacturing company as director of sales and marketing. He was new to the city and had moved from Detroit. I asked him if he was going to attend the big social event of the year. He said that his company was one of the corporate sponsors for the VIP tent. He asked if I was going to be there, and I told him that I was on my way to get my tickets. He said he looked forward to seeing me under the tent.

On that note, I stopped looking into his beautiful light brown eyes and down at my watch. *I am late!!!!!!* Oh my God, it was now 6:35 a.m. and I still had at least another ten minutes to drive to get to the center. I took his card and told him I had to go NOW! He laughed at my all-of-a-sudden need to rush, and told me to call him. I jumped into my car and headed downtown. I kept calling and *texting* Earline to make sure she had arrived at the ticket office, in line to get our tickets. I knew my girl was there in line.

When I was near the center, I saw a long line of cars trying to park in the parking garage. *Oh my God*, I thought. *These people are here to get tickets. I know my girl is in line and securing our VIP tickets.* When I finally parked the car, and walked what seem like a mile to the ticket office, I walked right past the long line of people to the front of the line, because I knew that was where my girl was. She was at the front of the line getting our tickets. Well, when I got to the front of the line and standing in front of the ticket counter, I didn't see her. I started to sweat and called her cell again. This time she picked up. I asked her, "Where are you, girl? I'm at the ticket office and I don't see you in line." She said that she stopped for gas, and because she knew that I was on my way, that I was probably at the center in line getting our tickets. Well, you know how this story ended. We didn't get a VIP ticket;

in fact, we didn't event get a regular ticket. Tickets sold out that morning.

My *CP Time* behavior, once again, **screwed me over**. I couldn't believe that I was late. I had planned and planned for this morning all year, and I was late. I missed out on going to the affair, and I missed out on seeing the good-looking brother who I had met at Starbucks who was going to be in the VIP tent looking for me. In my haste to get to the center, I must have dropped his business card, because I couldn't find it. Not only did being on *CP Time* screw up the biggest night of my life, *CP Time* also messed up my opportunity to meet "Mr. Right" again.

THE PET STORY

My dog was adopted because I was late getting to the dog shelter. I love my dog Rocky. He is my life. I don't have children, but I consider Rocky my child and I treat him like a child. He is spoiled rotten. He has toys, and two beds: one in my master bedroom, and one in his room, which is the laundry room. He goes to a doggy spa, and when I travel he stays at one of the best, most expensive doggy day care centers in the city. He even has a suite at the kennel so he doesn't have to sleep with the other dogs when he has an extended stay. He has clothes, beautiful collars with custom jewelry and his name on them. He even has a dog walker that comes to my house to make sure he gets his exercise when I have meetings all day.

I love my pet, and would do anything for him. For his birthday I gave him a birthday party and invited my friends with dogs to come over; our "children" ate doggy cake and played in the pool. It was a fabulous party that would go toe to toe with any real child's birthday party.

Rocky is my baby. He travels with me on the plane, not in the holding compartment, but he sits with me, in first class. I make sure that the hotels where I stay welcome pets. I enjoy taking him on vacations with me. He loves the beach, and I plan at least one vacation to the beach every year. Yes, I know, I am a doggy lover to the maximum.

This is my story: I also suffer from *CP Time*. *CP Time* is my middle name. I am always late for everything. I am never on time for anything. **I know I have a problem with being on time, and it has caused me major problems in my life.** But, one time, it almost caused Rocky to be gassed at the local humane society. *CP Time* almost cost me my pet. This is what happened:

One day Rocky got out of the backyard and started chasing a cat. My next-door neighbor saw him and called me to let me know that he was outside the fence. She told me that she had tried to call him, but he was trying to get to the other dog. She said she started to walk toward him but he started to run away and she didn't want to chase him away. When she called me she was frantic.

She, in fact everybody on my street and around the block, knew about Rocky, and how much I loved him. We would walk and my neighbors who saw us always stopped to pet him, or give him a treat. Many evenings we would stand in front of my friends' yards and talk while Rocky played with my friends' dogs, or sat by my feet bored.

I hung up the phone with her and ran out the front door. I started calling him by his name, but I didn't see him, nor did I hear him bark. This wasn't like him; he normally came running when I called, but not this time. So I jumped in my car and started driving around the neighborhood. I was getting worried, because I didn't see him. I asked people I saw walking or standing in their yards and no one had seen him. I was extremely worried by then, and called my brothers to come and help me find Rocky. My oldest brother, Mike, lived about a block away from me. He told me he would get his oldest son and start walking the streets looking for Rocky.

By now I had stopped several police cars and asked if they had seen him, and one of the officers suggested that I go to the dog shelter. I got the directions and headed down there to see if they had picked up Rocky. Well, to make a long story short, Rocky was picked up by the City Dog Catcher. They saw him running around and thought he was a stray and picked my baby up and put him in the back of the dog paddy wagon. He didn't have his on collar which had his tag. So he was just out and about with no ID tag to identify him as my pet. My poor baby was thrown in with the other common street mutts. They took Rocky to the dog shelter where he was booked as a runaway.

When I arrived he wasn't there but they told me to come in the next day to see if he would be brought in later that night. They closed at 7 p.m., but opened up at 9 a.m. The clerk told me that I needed to be there when they opened up to make sure that no one else would claim my dog. If he didn't have on a tag, anyone could claim him. That was the rule of this shelter. They had so many dogs that they were giving them away.

So I went home and worried myself, and anybody who would listen to death. I couldn't sleep knowing that Rocky could have been hit by a car or picked up by some dog thieves. I was sick, I could not sleep, I took a sleeping pill and lay down. I didn't know that it would knock me out; I thought it would just allow me to have a restful night. Well, it knocked me out and I didn't wake up until 11 a.m., and the only reason I woke up at 11 was my best friend stopped by to see how I was doing. When I realized how late it was, I was in a panic and told her to drive me to the dog shelter.

When we got there almost three hours after they opened, I found out that Rocky had been dropped off. A man had come in and told the staff Rocky was his dog, and he was given my baby. Because of arriving to the dog shelter on *CP Time*, my pet was now owned by a stranger. I did get my Rocky back. The staff gave me the new owner's name and when I told him my *CP Time* story of oversleeping, he understood and I picked up my baby. This taught me that when you need to be someplace on time, don't take any sleeping pills, because they will make you late and you will lose out. This is my *CP Time* story.

THE DOCTOR APPOINTMENT STORY

I hate to be late. I hate it when people make me late. I hate it when I have to wait on others who feel that my time is not important. They feel that they can just show up whenever they want to, and have no regard for people who are affected by their lack of time management.

I have two aunts and three uncles who are always late for family affairs. They show up at family gatherings hours after we have started. My Uncle Jim will show up sometimes four hours later and act like he's on time. I hate that. My favorite first cousin Kim will not even get dressed for church until I get to her house and outside blowing the car horn. She will have the nerve to stick her head out the door and tell me that she will be right out, knowing that she had not taken a shower. She is always late! I stopped picking her up for church, because by the time we got to church we had to park so far away that we had to get on the church parking lot shuttle to ride to the church. I hate sitting in the overflow section. That is the area for all the *CP Timers*, who didn't get to church on time to sit in the main sanctuary. We have to watch the big screen monitors. I hate that.

I hate it when I have an appointment with my doctor and she is late. One time that really stands out in my mind is when I actually waited for six hours, in the waiting room, because she was late.

When I got to the clinic, I signed in and was told to have a seat; my appointment was for 8 a.m. At 8:30 p.m. the nurse came and took me back to get the pre-check, and to take my blood. Then I was asked to have a seat in the exam room and the doctor would be right in. "Right in" is what the nurse said. That was at 9:00 a.m. At 9:45, I was still sitting on the exam table looking crazy. I had read all the outdated magazines that were in the room, I had played with the instruments, made some phone calls, and started getting nosey by reading all the brochures in the room about various medications and treatments. At 10:15 a.m., I lay on the exam table and almost fell asleep. At 10:30, I opened the exam room door and stuck my head out to see if I could get the attention of anyone to find out if they had forgotten about me.

I didn't see anyone so I grabbed the back of the exam gown so my ass wouldn't be exposed and walked toward the nurse's station. I saw a nurse sitting behind the desk and I asked her if the doctor was coming to check me, and how much longer would I have to wait.

The nurse looked up at me over her glasses and said, "Just be patient, the doctor is running a little late, but will be here soon."

RUNNING A LITTLE LATE! "You mean to tell me that she is not even here yet"? I screamed.

And the nurse said, "She will be here in a minute, just go back in the room and wait."

"WAIT...FOR HOW MUCH LONGER?" I shouted. I went off. I had been sitting in that room for damn near two hours and the doctor was not even in the building yet. A couple of other nurses and doctors heard me getting loud and came over to see if I needed to be sedated. I rolled my eyes at all of them as if to say, *Don't try me, or everybody in this clinic will be checking into a hospital for long term treatment from me putting my foot up some butts.*

I walked away from the nurse's desk, went back to the exam room, put my clothes on, and walked right out the door—right past the other waiting patients, past the front desk, and right through the door and to my car. As I get to the parking lot, guess who I run into? Dr. Reba Smith, a sister who saw me and said, **"Where are you going, don't we have an appointment?"**

I looked at her and started to go off, but instead I said very calmly, "I thought that when you control the health of a person that *CP Time* would not be a choice, and making me wait for over three hours was wrong. I will no longer use you as my doctor." I got in my car, and drove away. I didn't care at that time if I was terminally ill; *CP Time* had once again affected my life.

AN UNOFFICIAL SIN

CP Time behavior ruined my Service to God and my Church. I have always wanted to be up front and seen. I made sure that I was always chosen as the spokesperson for whatever I was involved with. I also have a problem with being on time. I was asked by my church to be the master of ceremonies for our Annual Men's Day Program. That meant I was required to make the program run smoothly, and even though I would not occupy a seat in the pulpit, I would be the main man for the program. I would be front and center.

The Sunday of the program I got out of bed, dressed in my new black suit with the gold tie and pocket square that was the official colors for Men's Day. I had gotten my hair cut on Saturday so I was fresh. I even stopped by my boy's spa, and had his girlfriend give me a pedicure and manicure. All well-dressed men know to finish off that polished look, and to be classified as well dressed you must have a manicure and a pedicure. Since I was going to be in front of the entire congregation I wanted to be on point. All the sisters would be checking me out, and there would be no question, I was *the man*.

I didn't want to be late. The pastor had asked me and the Men's Day committee to join him for a prayer breakfast in his private study. He informed me that the prayer breakfast was to begin at 7 a.m. He wanted all of the dedicated men who diligently worked on the program present at the breakfast. I was extremely proud to be among that list. In particular, he wanted the men who had raised over $50,000 to be his special guests to show his appreciation, and to get each *prayed up* for the long day ahead.

I was up and dressed by 6 a.m., and started up my car. This morning it was cold outside and it had snowed the night before, but my car was in the garage so I didn't have to worry about cleaning it off. The streets were covered, but not too bad. I would be okay and shouldn't have any major problems getting to the church. I had hoped that Deacon Leroy had gotten to the church and cleared the parking lot and the sidewalk. We usually had a snow removal service to clean the parking lot, but this was the first snowfall of the season, and the trustees of the church had not secured the snow removal service for the winter season. It was still snowing, but the sun was out and the sky was a beautiful deep blue.

I put on my coat, turned on the house alarm and got in my car. I turned it on and opened up the garage door. While the car warmed up, I decided to go back into the house and make a pot of coffee. I had given up other "medicinal beverages," but I had yet to give up coffee. I had plenty of time to make a pot and still make it to the church in plenty of time for the prayer breakfast.

As I was making a pot of coffee, I decided to get on line and check out some web sites. Something else I had not given up, the Internet, however that is another story. I usually use the Internet for my business. I work in real estate; I try to stay on top of my business, and the Internet is a great tool to post and get new listings. I use it to find out what houses are on the market.

I checked out the new listings, and lost track of time. Anyone who uses the Internet knows how you can get deeper and deeper into the web sites. When I realized that I had been surfing the net for over an hour, my car had run out of gas, while in the garage and I was too late to get to the church by seven. It was now 7:15 a.m., and I live twenty minutes from the church without any problems. That means no snow, no traffic, and no slow drivers. There is no way that I could make it to the church now. I was out of gas and it was still snowing. If I had just gotten into the car and left the house when I had planned, I would not have been in this situation. I called the church office, but no one answered. I was screwed. I knew the pastor was upset with me and my committee was probably talking about me always being late.

I finally got my sister to pick me up on her way to church. When we got there the 11 a.m. service was starting and the men were in place, everyone but me. When I walked to the back of the church, I ran in to my co-chairman of the Men's Day Program. He looked at me and said, **"Boy, Jesus is not going to wait on you when Judgment Day comes when He comes back for the saints."** He started laughing.

I felt so bad, and for the rest of the day, everybody teased me about always being on *CP Time*. Even the pastor made a comment during the sermon about people who are late, and how that lateness is considered an unofficial sin, and God likes order. I will never be late again for anything; I learned my lesson this time. CP and God do not mix.

CP TIME DESTROYED AN AFTERNOON OF SEX!

I **am a freak.** I know I am. I love making love to my lady. We can do it several times a day, every day. She knows how to rock my world and I know how to make her beg me not to stop. Yea, we got it going on like that, but there is only one problem. We can't be on time to make love. We both are chronic *CP Timers*. Either she is late getting home because she always has to stop at the store, or her girlfriend's house, or she will tell me to be ready to *get some* and she doesn't show up until two hours later, and I have fallen asleep waiting on her *always on CP Time ass.*

One time we made plans to take the afternoon off from work and meet just to *freak*. We were going to *freak* all afternoon. I told her to meet me at the house at 2 p.m. sharp. She said she would be there and to be ready. I told her that I would have everything ready and all she had to do is walk in, come upstairs to the bedroom, *and get on it*. She said that was what she needed, just for me to have my way with her. So the day we were going to spend all day *freaking*, I took off work at 11 a.m., and headed to the house. I cleaned up the house, changed the sheets, put some fresh cut flowers in a vase on the bed table, and took a long, long, hot bath. I timed myself to be out of the tub, oiled down and smelling good at 1:50 p.m., just in time for her to walk in and see her man, all ready and smelling good. At 1:50 p.m. I was already in the bed. The sheets were pulled back, the drapes were drawn, and I was butt naked. I put on our favorite CD, and just *laid back* ready for my lady to step through the bedroom door for an afternoon of pure pleasure.

At 2:15 she was not home, but she called to let me know that she was stuck in traffic. She told me that she was on her way and had already taken off her panties so she wouldn't have to waste any time getting on her favorite man. I believed her, and I tried not to say anything about her always being late. We had some fights in the past about her always being late. In fact, she was a teacher and her principal had warned her that if she was late one more time to school, she would be put on probation. She and I had stopped speaking, after she made me late for a very important family event. My family talked about her like a dog behind her back, because she was always late. But, the time my parents invited us to my favorite aunt and uncle's seventy-fifth wedding anniversary and we didn't get there until after they blew out the candles on the cake and I missed my toast to them, I almost filed for divorce...reason: *CP TIME*.

But this afternoon, I put all of that behind me and all I wanted was my baby on top of me, riding me like a professional call girl. At 2:45

p.m., I had gotten up to get a bottle of water. I was no longer in an excited state...if you know what I mean. I mean, a brother can only maintain his hard-on but for so long.

I looked out the front window to see if I could spot her driving down our street. I called her, but she didn't pick up. I didn't get upset, I just went back upstairs and got back in the bed and turned on the television. At 3:30 p.m., I was now dressed and headed out the door. This woman had done it to me again. I couldn't believe that she was not home and had not called. As I walked toward my car, she pulled up. I had that *pissed off pissed on* look in my eyes. She jumped out the car, and ran up to me and hugged me. **She asked me where was I going, and what happened to our afternoon of making crazy love.**

I pushed her away from me and asked her in a very loud tone, "Where in the hell have you been?" It was now 4:30 p.m., and I had been waiting on her butt since 2 p.m.

She looked at me and said, "I had to stop and get a wax. I didn't want to scratch you up, so I stopped at Miss Ling Ling's and had her give me a full body wax."

"A freakin' body wax!" I screamed. "You made me wait all afternoon for you while you got a freakin' body wax!"

I told her that her late *CP*-living behind was not going to screw up my life. I jumped in my car, and sped down the street. She just stood there looking silly. I didn't call her, and when I did come back home, I slept in the guest room with the door locked. She could take her bikini wax and do herself with it, maybe then she wouldn't play with my time ever again. And she didn't.

LATE PRETTY BOY

I **am known in my family for my lateness**. It is certainly not from the apple tree. My father was never late and he was also well organized. Which leads me to question if I am, in fact, his first-born-male child. I have none of his qualities or looks. He was a short stout dark manly man. I am tall, thin and what they call a pretty boy, that's what they call me, pretty boy. As a matter of fact, they call me LPB, Late Pretty Boy. I am always late and everyone around me knows it. I must admit I have no regard for those around me when I am late, on purpose. It is quite necessary that I make a grand entrance everywhere I go. I would hate to deprive men and women the opportunity to see pretty boy make a grand entrance, always dressed to the nines and arriving in my 2006 black on black Hummer.

I can recall one particular time when I was extremely late, but as usual, I thought, **the party does not begin until LPB arrives. Wrong! Ouch!** Not only did the party start without me the location of the event had been moved. I had no prior notice of this. When I arrived at the event a note on the door gave an address that was a good fifteen minutes away, this was on a good day.

However, the day seemed to be the busiest day of the year. The Atlanta Braves had a home game. The game was over, and I was caught up in the traffic. By the time I arrived at the social function everyone was leaving. LPB rolled up in his black on black Hummer and rolled out, but not so smoothly, everyone saw me as they left honking their horns. I couldn't hide in my dinosaur of a vehicle. Needless to say my friends and family did not let me live that one down.

LATE FOR AN EXAM

I am a proud to be a black self-made, successful real estate broker in the Midwest. There are very few of us. I pride myself on my successful business. The only area that I am lacking perfection in is my tardiness. I attribute this to my AADD; it has proven to be both a blessing and a curse. My AADD keeps me moving, but it also causes me late to be to my appointments.

Promptness is necessary in this business. Any businessperson will tell you to be on time—before time—to your appointments. The competition is quite strong; there is no room for sloppy performance, and especially lateness.

I learned this lesson during recertification for my Brokers License. The exam had already been in session for the first half of the day. I knew that my promptness for the exam was imperative; I was half an hour early in the morning for the first session. Of course as I grew tired throughout the day, my ability to focus and stay on point grew increasingly difficult.

Lunch was about to begin. I decided that I needed a serious break from the monotonous exam. I opted to sneak away from the rest of the group taking the exam, and not eat with them in the designated cafeteria at the testing site. I would have my lunch at a popular restaurant close to the building. Downtown rush hour was not at all like my small town; this was not a noon rush hour, this was a traffic jam.

Prior to lunch we had a fifteen-minute break and I used that opportunity to network with my colleagues. I had met one individual whom I quickly established a rapport. You learn in this business, or any business, the importance of networking; it would later prove to be an asset.

Lunch was over, I always kept my watch set fifteen minutes early, because I knew my problem with AADD and being late. I was not too worried. Since my watch was set to give me a fifteen lead time and allows me to arrive early to appointments, this afternoon everything was going perfect. decided to head back to the institute where the exam was being given. As I pulled out the parking lot and onto the street, I realized that I didn't have my cell phone on my hip. It must have fallen off, or I sat it on the table while I ate lunch. So I pulled over and did a U-turn to go back to find my phone. I was okay, I was not close to being late, so I was not stressed over the time.

When I got back to the restaurant, I parked my car, got out and walked toward where I had sat for lunch. I didn't see the phone, so I asked the waitress and she told me she didn't see it. Then I started asking other people in the restaurant if they had noticed a cell phone. No one had. I then asked a young man if he would call my phone. Maybe if it rang, then I could locate it. As he called my number, I remembered I had put it on vibrate. I stated getting a little nervous, because I need my phone. So, I started backtracking my steps to find my phone. I forgot all about the time. I needed my phone, I had no regard for the time that passed; I needed my lifeline, my cell phone.

After a period of time, I decided it was lost or someone had picked it up. So, I headed back to the car. When I got to my car, I noticed that there was a police officer writing me a ticket for parking on a yellow line. *Damn.* I walked up to him and asked him if he would not write the ticket, because of my urgency to get my phone that I had lost. He dismissed my plea, and continued to write the ticket. He took his time and by now, I was over an hour late to the exam center. So, when I did finally arrive, I was not admitted back into the classroom to continue the exam, and was dismissed due to returning from lunch on *CP Time.*

I lost my pride, my cell phone, and my broker's license.

ALZHEIMER'S MADE MY WEDDING LATE

The day began with a brilliant bright sunrise peering out over the tall buildings of the city, as I stood on the terrace of my tenth-floor apartment thanking God for such a beautiful day. Ecstatic that it was finally here, my wedding day, the telephone rang to interrupt my thoughts. It was my husband-to-be; I liked using "husband-to-be" instead of "fiancé," I enjoyed hearing the sound of the word "husband."

My husband-to-be was on the phone in a panic: "We have lost Grandpa!" He shouted it again. The cell phone connection was weak; his voice was fading in and out. I thought he meant Grandpa had died. I began by saying, "We can postpone the wedding until after his funeral." After I finally stopped talking to listen to what he was saying, and the call became clear again, I realized he had kept trying to interrupt me to explain Grandpa had not died. Grandpa had walked away from the hotel room my parents had rented for my husband's grandparents during our wedding weekend.

His grandmother had taken her shower thinking Grandpa was still asleep; he was in the bed when she had gotten into the shower. When she had finished her shower, she planned to wake Grandpa, and assist with bathing him and getting him dressed and ready for the wedding, which was her daily routine. She went to wake Grandpa and he wasn't in the hotel room. My future in-laws were in the room next to my husband's grandparents. My grandmother banged on their door to alert them.

This was not the first time Grandpa had walked away, but it had only been for a few moments during the day, and he was in Grandma's eyesight.

The family had been looking for Grandpa for the last three hours. I scolded my fiancé for not alerting me sooner. He said he did not want me to worry, I wanted a perfect wedding day. I explained that his grandparents were more important than that.

After looking throughout the hotel and the hotel grounds for his grandfather, the hotel personnel also assisted. The manager finally suggested that the family call the local police station. We were glad that we called and so happened a woman had spotted Grandpa at a lake with his pajamas on feeding the ducks. This is something that he always did at home, at the lake when he was a child. The woman had convinced Grandpa to get into her car "to get more food for the ducks," she had told him. He went along with her, unknowingly, to the police station. We were blessed for that particular lady to find him rather than someone who meant him harm.

Our wedding started an hour late because of the early morning fiasco. They had begun looking for him at 9 a.m., and found him at the police station at noon. The wedding was an hour late. It was to begin at 1:30 and did not begin until 2:30. **One of my bridesmaids overheard the guests start to murmur about expecting that the wedding would be late because black folk can never start a wedding on time.** I ignored the murmurs. I was elated that we still had Grandpa, and my wedding day was the happiest day of my life.

HUSBAND LATE—MAN IN THE MIRROR

I **called my sister to ask why they had not arrived at the dinner.** It was Thanksgiving Day and she had prepared the turkey, stuffing, and gravy. It was already an hour past three; this was the time that we had agreed upon. We know our entire family is notorious for being late, however, my sister and her husband are always, always, extremely late.

If a bet had been made that day for who would be late, everyone would have put their money on them. We make it a practice to agree on an early time for our family dinners to begin two hours before we actually wish to eat, to ensure that she and her husband will be on time. It never fails every time I invite my sister and her husband to anything they are late. My sister finally admitted it's her husband who makes them late. I called to see if I could hurry them along.

"Girl, I am dressed and ready, but Pretty Boy is still in the mirror."

I slammed the phone down. Everyone was ready to eat. Uncle Jim was about to go into a diabetic coma from not eating; everyone else was famished. Lord knows, we could have all probably skipped the turkey, but on Thanksgiving Day! I drove over to their house to retrieve the turkey. My sister let me in and I headed straight for her kitchen to get the bird. Her husband came down the stairs with shaving cream on his face and his robe on, with his hair clippers in his hand. At the same time he asked my sisters if she would cut the hairs in his ears.

I yelled from the kitchen, "Who cares if you have hairs in your ears. We need to have dinner so Uncle Jim can eat. He is about to slip into a coma!" I mumbled, "People have no regard for others."

My sister packed the bird, and put on her coat and left her house with me. Her husband never came to Thanksgiving dinner.

I have asked several of my girlfriends and co-workers what makes them late most of the time. They all answered their husbands or male friends. They claim the men in their life spend more time in the mirror than they do. My girlfriends say their men primp more, and constantly make them late.

SEMINAR BEGAN ON CP TIME

I was to be the guest speaker at an event in a major city at an Historically Black College (HBCU). I pride myself on being on time; since I'm black it seems I'm expected to be late. I go out of my way to always arrive early. On this particular occasion I was disappointed that my escort arrived forty minutes after the event was to begin, to drive me to the event. My escort was chairman of the Sociology Department of the university, and held two doctorate degrees, one in human behavior. I was appalled by his tardiness.

We finally arrived at the venue; the crowd was slim with only a handful of people. I thought the people had left because of my tardiness. I really felt bad, however, I later found out it wasn't my tardiness that made everyone leave. No one had showed up.

The professor was actually waiting for more people to arrive before bringing me to an empty auditorium. He was under the assumption that the black people were always late and would begin filing in late. The people never showed. He later found out that the event was not advertised in the local media, as his assistant had claimed. The news releases were not sent out by the required deadlines of the local media. **If you advertise on time, they will come.**

IN CHURCH

Not only does *CP Time* in black churches start late, you stay late no matter what time you start. *CP Time* will wear you out, especially if you go to church. If you are at a white church, church will begin at seven and you are guaranteed to get out by eight. One hour and out. **A black church service will keep you all night.** The testimony service will last an hour, the preacher still has to preach, and the choir will sing A, B, C, and D selections.

I have several white friends who I have invited to my church. They all came the first time I invited them, but none of them have made a return visit. I have asked each of them, and they all say my church services are too long.

BAD HABITS

Some habits are just hard to break, and being late is one of them. When I was working at my first corporate job right out of college, I found myself meeting a goal that I had set for myself to reach when I knew that I would graduate from college. I had some bumps in my road toward acquiring my bachelor of science in communications from Central State University. CSU is located outside of Dayton, Ohio and the students are known for partying rather than studying. I should say *some* students.

Well, to keep it real, I was one of the students who helped give CSU that reputation. I partied every night of the week, and the weekends were non-stop drinking, smoking, chasing the fine sisters on campus, and even doing my thing in Xenia, Ohio, a small city located right outside the campus.

Man, me, and my *boys* had a place off campus, and were known as the party dogs. Everybody came to our house parties. They would remind you of the *House Party* movies of the early '90s fame. Well, all of this partying really hurt my grades and put me on probation a couple of semesters due to my overindulgence. I didn't take my classes seriously, and it cost me. I didn't get serious until my senior year.

My dad and mom told me that if I didn't graduate from CSU on time, they would cut me off. That meant, the car would be repossessed by my dad, my credit card would be cancelled, and I would be forced to return home to Birmingham, Alabama, to work on my grandfather's farm for the rest of my life—and that was not an option for me.

I had seen all of my cousins and uncles slave on the family farm, and I had spent most of my summers working on the farm. I was not going to end up like my family members who thought making good pay and busting your ass was the American way.

So I had to change my ways. I hired a tutor, a fine redbone sister from the Virgin Islands, who was feeling me. She let me know that I could have that "ass" whenever I wanted it. I called her one afternoon and told her that I needed her. She thought that I wanted to get with her between the sheets, when in fact, the only sheets I needed to get at were sheets of the pages of my books.

Sheila was her name, and we started meeting every day at the library. I had not spent that much time at the library, but it soon became my second home. She was a hard taskmaster, and made sure that I studied hard. She made sure that I didn't go to one party, and she even told my roommates that if they had a party, I was not allowed to attend, and they should put me out of the house the nights or weekends when they threw a party. They respected her and didn't want her to tell all the sisters on campus that they were just what the newspapers said about young black men—they were lazy, sorry, and didn't care about their futures. They gave her their support to help me get through these trying days so I could graduate on time.

Sheila would tell me not to be late for our scheduled times to meet and study. If I was five minutes late, she would not be there. She would leave. She taught me that *CP Time* was something that she would not stand for, and anyone who was late, was in her mind, lower then dirt. I learned to not be late for our study sessions.

Well, to make a long story short, I did graduate on time, thanks to Sheila's help. So now I am sitting in my new office looking out the window of my forty-fifth-floor office. The Mead Paper Company located in downtown Dayton, Ohio recruited me. This was perfect as my first job right out of school. I was close to my boys who were still at CSU, due to their partying, and I could still participate in the parties without having to worry about classes and studying. But one bad habit that still was part of me was being late.

During the new employee orientation, we were told that if you clocked in five minutes past your start time, you would be considered late. If you are late more than five times in any pay period, you could be terminated, and if you are late more then two times during the ninety-day probation period, that was grounds for instant termination. We had to sign the form stating that we understood the policies of being late. I knew this was going to be an issue for me, but I was going to do my best to not be late. Hell, I was making $65,000 per year. And I had just leased a new 325i black on black BMW. I was going to be the envy of all my "still in college" boys. I could and would not mess this up. My parents were proud of me and they bragged to everybody in the family every chance they got about their son being a college-educated, corporate-working, young upwardly mobile brother who was going to be the president of the company one day. They were proud of me and I was happy that they were happy.

The first week at my new job went smooth. I arrived at the orientation class every day on time; sometimes I would be the first in the room. Starting the second week, we were required to work in the factory, and the shift started at 5 a.m. That was a bitch. I knew getting up at 4 a.m. to arrive at the factory by 5 a.m. was going to be rough. The week I was required to work at the factory I went to bed at 9 p.m., I set my clock alarm to go off at 3 a.m., and I made sure that my clothes were laid out so I could just roll out of bed, jump in the shower and head out.

Things don't always go the way you want them to go. The second day of the 5 a.m. shift didn't go as I had planned. First, I overslept because I went out for a beer with one of my former classmates who begged me to see her, because she was having some problems with her boyfriend who was a friend of mine. Then my clock didn't go off, because I forgot to set it. I was extremely tired when I got back to my apartment. I wasn't thinking. When I woke up, it was 5:45 a.m. I panicked and by the time I got dressed and to the factory, it was 6:50 a.m. Not good. I did not punch the time clock. Instead I went straight to the foreman's office. When I got there, my supervisor was on the phone and looked up at me with this look on his face that worried me. It was not a good look, it was a look of disapproval. I sat down in the lobby and looked at the clock. The time was now 7:15 a.m. The crew was already on their first ten-minute break of the morning. I had really messed up.

When Mr. Wright finally got off the phone, he asked me to come into this office. I went in, and as soon as I sat down, I started telling him how sorry I was for being late and that I had to help out a friend, and on and on. I must have sounded like a babbling fool.

He just sat back and listened to me. When I stopped, he said, "Son, you need to understand that in the real world, that you are now a part of, **excuses are just like buttholes, everybody has one**. But, at Mead Paper Company, we only want the best, brightest, and people who value their time, and the time of the company. It is now 7:30 a.m., and you, young man, are so late, that it is costing the company money, you money, and me money. Time is lost forever. We at Mead don't need people who are late and especially people who are late in their first two weeks. I am going to report this to the human resources office and they will contact you. Go to your group and get to work."

Later that day I got a call from Human Resources informing me that due to my serious lateness my job was terminated. I was fired for being on *CP Time*. My future, my car, my apartment, my life was over. I didn't know what I would tell my folks and my friends. I finally did tell them that I got fired because I was late, and that it cost me a good job and a bright future. *CP Time* strikes again, and this time it impacted more people than just me.

SHIFTING GEARS

If my husband will be late, he would rather not go. I have repeatedly made my husband late to numerous functions. He has finally grown tired of being late because of me. He decided he would one day "teach me a lesson on being on time." This happened when I least expected; it was his plan to take it to the next level.

We had been invited to a barbecue at a close friend's nephew's house. We lived in Universal City, Texas, and our friend's nephew lived in San Antonio, on the west side. We were located east of San Antonio. It was a good thirty-minute drive to his house.

As usual I had to prepare the potato salad, and bake a pie. I made the best potato salad and homemade pies; they were in demand, and I had promised our friend's nephew my specialties. I always prepared my food from scratch so it takes some time for me to cook.

My husband said to me the night before, "You know how long it takes you to make potato salad, and homemade apple pie. Don't you think you had better make it tonight ahead of time, so that we will be on time for the barbecue?"

I replied with my usual, "I will get up early in the morning to cook," knowing I was already exhausted from planting flowers that day.

Of course I overslept, and had not put the pie in the oven. It would take a good two hours to bake. This time I was baking a deep-dish cobbler. It took forty-five minutes just to put the pie together. Dough from scratch was no joke. I still had to make the potato salad; that meant cutting up the potatoes, and cooking them, boiling the eggs, cutting the onion, etc. My time was limited; Murphy knew this (Murphy's Law). The potatoes overboiled, making them mushy, so I put them in the refrigerator for mashed potatoes later. I had to wash, peel, and cook more potatoes.

My husband was playing with my daughter, and watching baseball on television while I cooked. He wouldn't lift a finger to help me, part of his lesson, since he had suggested that I cook the night before.

It was now time to get dressed for the barbecue, and my husband gets our daughter and himself ready. This is after asking me to find his socks, and my daughter's favorite red shoes. Of course they were where they were supposed to be, but he couldn't seem to find them. This was a distraction from my cooking, Murphy again. I forgot to put the eggs in the potato salad and when I peeled one it was not done, so I had to, you guessed it, make more.

Finally I got everything prepared, with a half-hour left for the pie to bake. My husband said he couldn't wait on me, that it was time to go, if we wanted to be on time. Of course, the pie was still in the oven, and I wasn't dressed yet. He left with my daughter, after saying, "You can drive to the barbecue when you get ready." I realized, after a few minutes, that he took the car that I normally drove. The other car, his car, was a stick shift, a manual transmission. I didn't know how to drive a stick shift! Boy, was I angry. I thought, *you @$$ #*%&!*

My husband had taken me out for a couple of lessons, but he did not have the patience to teach me and I was easily frustrated. So I had never gotten the hang of driving a manual. I was in a huff, and by this time he was at the barbecue. I called our friend's house and asked to speak with my husband. I yelled over the phone, "Why did you take my car?"

"Your car!" he yelled back. "Our car, if you want to come to the barbecue you will have to drive our other car, or stay at home." He knew full well that I could not drive a manual shift.

I heard our friend in the background say, "Man, where is your *little woman*, and my pie?" Well, this "little woman" was not going to stay at home because she could not drive a stick shift.

The food was ready, and I was now dressed. I did not wait for the pie to cool off. I packed the food, put it in the stick shift, said a prayer, and took off, with the clutch grinding. Oh boy, that was the ride of my life. But I was determined to learn that day, to teach my husband a lesson that you cannot keep a good *little woman* down. I did not care how much it cost to replace the clutch. Then I got the hang of it. I remembered my husband had told me, "Let off easy on the clutch, and shift." I was riding relatively smoothly until I approached the HILL!

I had never seen an entrance ramp that was a steep hill. Okay, maybe it wasn't that steep, but in a manual car, it was steep. I looked behind me to see if there were any cars. No, I was home free if I rolled backward. So I came to a stop. There was a stop sign instead of a yield sign to enter the highway traffic. *How am I supposed to get my momentum going on a hill, after a complete stop, and enter this highway traffic?* I was talking to my self, and to God.

"Help me, God!" I tried to put it in first gear but rolled back down the hill. I tried again and got messed up, and the car cut off. I started the car, and this time I got to second gear. There was now a car behind me.

"Lord, it's me and you." I said a quick prayer, rolled the window down, and stuck my head out to get the attention of the other driver. "I am not good at driving a stick," I yelled. "Would you please move back?" She smiled as if she understood, waved her hand and backed up giving me enough room if I should roll backward.

I tried again, angry, scared, and determined to get to my destination. To my surprise I got up the hill. God must have cleared the way for me. There was no approaching traffic on the highway. That hill taught me all I needed to know about driving a manual. I was home free. "Thank you, God, and thank you, lady."

Needless to say when I got to the barbecue, my husband was shocked, and so were his friends. Evidently he had told them he had left me with the manual shift car, and I would probably not make the barbecue. My husband's back was turned when I walked into the backyard with the pie in my hand, and a big smirk on my face.

Our friend yelled, **"Well, it looks like I will get my pie after all! But it looks like you, my friend, will be wearing yours,"** he said, referring to my husband.

"Ooh baby, I see you made it." His voice shook as he was expecting me to throw the pie on him. Instead I went right past him to my girlfriends, and began to brag about how I had mastered the manual. My daughter gave me a big hug and said, "I knew you would get here, I am so proud of you, Mommy."

I was on *CP Time* that day, but it was to my advantage. I learned to drive a stick that day, and gained new respect from my husband, and our friend. I never heard them call me *little woman* after that, and I now try to prepare the night before.

SURPRISE BIRTHDAY PARTY STARTED LATE

I **have never been to a surprise birthday party that began late.** The guest of honor was already at the party, and all of the guests had not arrived. His wife had purposefully added to the invitations, *Please be on time. It is a surprise party.*

When the guests had not arrived, his wife kept him in the parking lot of the hotel. She had a friend who had arrived on time to distract him with a problem with his car. People continued to arrive while he was assisting the friend with his car. He thought they were just going to dinner in the hotel restaurant with the other couple.

Finally the majority of the guests had arrived and the party favors were in place. The friend took him into the party room of the hotel, and everyone yelled, "Surprise!' He later said he wondered why so many people were entering the hotel that he knew personally.

LATE FOR CHURCH

T**here are so many instances of blatant tardiness in my past, present, and most likely, my future.** The one thing I can't quite wrap my mind around is the fact that my mother was late for church on Sundays, for YEARS, and she is the Minister of Music, and has been for decades! She used to come in with an attitude, practically glaring at the congregation like she was saying, **"Yeah, I'm late. You got a problem wit' that?"** (she's all of five-foot-one on a good day.) Well, she's no longer late because I, her baby girl, teach women's Sunday School on Sunday mornings. So she comes in early and we have a marvelous time during our classes.

Following Sunday School, she has time to go to the undercroft, partake of the breakfast that is served, and still be at her piano when church starts. So, my teaching Sunday School has solved this problem for her, and I don't think that much of anything else would have done it. Actually, this is the first time I have really thought about it! Once again, God has proven Himself to be so GOOOOOOD.

LATE MAIL/TRASH LATE IN A BLACK NEIGHBORHOOD

Maybe this is not quite *CP Time* at its true definition, however, in my neighborhood, we live across tracks. The railroad tracks are the physical division of the "haves and have nots" in my city as it is in other cities in the United States. The railroad tracks used to separate black people and white people; now they separate classes of people. I remember when I was a little girl, my mother and father did not allow me to venture across the tracks, or walk downtown without permission, and a destination.

It seems now the division in our city means you will be left behind with the city services, trash pickup the last day of the week, mail delivery at six in the evening, no pizza delivery in my neighborhood, street cleaning, snow removal (on bad winter days that can make you late for work, it's not our fault), etc.

My sister's theory on this is: Black folk, from slavery on, had to be last in line, and last to receive anything. A prime example of this is some black people, not all black people, but a lot of black folk enjoy eating chitlins. However, I am not one of them. They have acquired a taste for the scrap of the animal, because it was the leftover. We had to take what the white man did not want to eat, the last of the hog. We got the last of the crop. We had to stand in line last, sit in the last seat of the bus and in the last train car, and be last to get hired. We wait to be the last served in restaurants. Note some of these mentioned "lasts" are still happening today. After we were allowed to read, we got the used textbooks from the white schools, after they were worn and outdated (not so long ago for some schools I might add).

This is my sister's theory on why black folk are always late and last; we can't help it. It is ingrained in black folks' subconscious to wait and be last.

CONCLUSION

A myth to some and a reality to most, Colored People's time is a silent killer, it never fails. Known as *"CP Time"* to many, the African American trend of being more than fashionably late has been around for decades. No matter the event or social setting, any gathering can and will fall victim to *CP Time*. Many a wedding, graduation, performance and funeral have been missed or started late because of *CP Time*. Although arriving late to such functions as important as these are usually not funny at the time, in retrospect all we can do is shake our head at the ridiculousness and pervasiveness of the problem.

While some people in the African American community regard the phenomenon as a stereotype, *CP Time* is a trend that is practiced, even if unintentionally, by many African Americans. Despite the fact that not many people are prepared to declare the problem is genetic and ingrained in African American culture, no one has yet been able to explain the inclination for African Americans to habitually be late. Some people believe that *colored people's time* will become increasingly problematic for future generations that will have to continue the fight for racial equality in America. There are fears that *CP Time* will become another excuse for people to discriminate against Blacks in this country, and their fears might one day be realized.

An alternative view of *CP Time* is that it is a hilarious cultural stigma. This book is an in-depth observation of the many good and sometimes bad reasons Black folk are almost never on time. Comprised of stories from people from every walk of life, *CP Time* makes light of the reasons why people are often late and undoubtedly provides amusing situations that every reader will be able to relate to. You are invited to judge for yourself.

Noted professor
Morehouse College
Atlanta, GA

ABOUT THE AUTHOR

J. L. King is a *New York Times* best-selling author of *On the Down Low* and *Essence* best-seller of *Coming up from the Down Low*, philanthropist, publisher, educator, community activist, businessman and producer.

He was named one of the top 50 most Intriguing African Americans for 2004 in the November issue of *Ebony* magazine and has appeared on the Oprah Winfrey show and on over 300 TV and radio shows, including the cover of *Jet* magazine in 2004.

He is currently working with writers who aspire to become authors through his Write Your Way Through literary workshops and conferences. His passion to teach African American writers on how to become published authors is his way of giving back.

He currently resides in Atlanta, GA and has three adult children and two beautiful grandsons.

To learn more about his workshops, visit www.jlking.net or www. myspace.com/jameslking.

Reasons Why I'm Always Late

People In My Life Who Are Late

My Plan to Start Being On Time